施璐德亚洲有限公司 编

施璐德年鉴 2018

VISION
DRIVEN
LIFE

CNOOD 2008 TO 2018

复旦大學 出版社

图书在版编目(CIP)数据

施璐德年鉴.2018/施璐德亚洲有限公司编.—上海：复旦大学出版社，2019.7
ISBN 978-7-309-14353-9

Ⅰ.①施… Ⅱ.①施… Ⅲ.①建筑企业-上海-2018-年鉴 Ⅳ.①F426.9-54

中国版本图书馆 CIP 数据核字(2019)第 097130 号

施璐德年鉴.2018
施璐德亚洲有限公司 编
责任编辑/谢同君

复旦大学出版社有限公司出版发行
上海市国权路 579 号 邮编：200433
网址：fupnet@fudanpress.com http://www.fudanpress.com
门市零售：86-21-65642857 团体订购：86-21-65118853
外埠邮购：86-21-65109143 出版部电话：86-21-65642845
上海丽佳制版印刷有限公司

开本 787×1092 1/16 印张 14.5 字数 309 千
2019 年 7 月第 1 版第 1 次印刷

ISBN 978-7-309-14353-9/F·2576
定价：88.00 元

如有印装质量问题,请向复旦大学出版社有限公司出版部调换。
版权所有　　侵权必究

序　言
Preface

■ Benjamin Tam

诚获施璐德亚洲有限公司池勇海董事长邀请，为施璐德年鉴二零一八撰写序言，余深感荣幸。池董事长，学不厌，诲不倦。士不可不弘毅，任重而道远。创立施璐德学会，致力探究中华传统文化，肩挑传承慧命之大任。年鉴集里明真意，堪慰年来教学心。更欣知此年鉴内的文章，为公司内部各员工之深彻体会与心路历程之慷慨分享，各撰业卷，舒其所得，实在别具意义。

I feel greatly honored to be invited by Dennis, Chairman of CNOOD ASIA LIMITED, to write a preface to *CNOOD Yearbook 2018*. Dennis is a person who learns without flagging and teaches without growing weary. "A gentleman must be strong and resolute, for his burden is heavy and the road is long." As the founder of the CNOOD Society, Dennis devotes himself to exploring Chinese traditional culture, taking on the responsibility of inheriting the life of wisdom. In the *Yearbook*, one will see a true meaning, which amply consoles the heart of a teacher. I am also glad to learn that all the articles in this *Yearbook* have been written by members of the CNOOD family, in which they generously share their deep understanding and mental journey, as well as what they have benefited from working with CNOOD. There is really something special about it.

此年鉴内的文章内容，蕴含了先古圣贤无穷智慧的运用。执古之道，以御今之有。皆源于施璐德公司文化，好古敏求，业精于勤，立身接物，功在社会。当中包含了能力、勇气、志向、应用方法、创新思维和远大的目光等元素，皆现代社会所需的宝贵特质，亦是对现今职场工作人员的启发，令人受益匪浅。

安土敦乎仁，故能爱。在施璐德公司，更可感见其鼓励尽性之心，到达了极致。这仁爱并非在工作岗位上安于现状，而是在当前环境下，进德修业，努力做到最好。既有诚信，又能坚而不越，执德不移，所行必有功也。但纸上得来终觉浅，绝知此事要躬行，而非经一番寒彻骨，哪得梅花扑鼻香。如未能笃行不倦，只旁观世外风光，或以指为月、或断章取义、或迷于文字，都只如水中捉月，终无入处。衷心感谢施璐德公司诸君，在学业、工作和家庭事务奔波劳碌之余，不畏道路之遥，风雨之阻，不遗余力，撰写引导文章，引而伸之，授业解惑，出于至诚，其心可佩。

In these articles we see the application of the infinite wisdom of ancient sages. Adhering to the time-honored Way we deal with business in the present-day world. It all comes from the corporate culture of CNOOD, which is about being fond of fine tradition and earnestly seeking it, achieving superior performance by diligence, conducting yourself and dealing with others, with the aim of making contributions to the society. This corporate culture are made up of elements including ability, courage, ambition, applicable methodology, creative thinking and lofty vision, all of which should be considered as precious qualities in modern society. People today in the business can also be inspired by it and benefit a lot from it.

As is said in the *Book of Changes*, "He rests in his own position, and cherishes the spirit of generous benevolence; and hence he can love." At CNOOD, we are more strongly aware of the supreme extent to which the company encourages people to fully develop their potentials. By "benevolence" and "love" we do not mean being idle at your work and feeling comfortable with things as they are; you have to make progress in your virtue and business, trying to do your best. With sincerity and trust, you will definitely achieve something in what you do if you are resolute enough and unswervingly principled. On the other hand, however, what you learn by books is after all superficial; only by practice can you

集而锡号"施璐德年鉴"。文皆及义，余得先睹之快。索序于余，恳辞不许；唯不揣谫陋，勉諉数言，聊以塞责，草以为序！

gain a thorough knowledge of things. As the Chinese saying goes, "Without the bitter cold, how shall we have the rich fragrance of the plum blossom?" If you fail to practice devotedly and tirelessly, being only a spectator outside the world, who mistakes the finger pointing to the moon for the moon itself, understands things out of context, or is obsessed with words and letters, it will be like trying to catch the moon in the water:—you can never find out where to begin with. Here I would like to express my heartfelt gratitude to people from CNOOD ASIA LIMITED, who, while busy in their daily work and life, do not fear the long road or any obstacles and spare no effort in writing these instructive articles, in which they further expound and help to solve our perplexity. They do it out of pure sincerity and should be held in esteem.

Such a collection of articles is then entitled *CNOOD Yearbook*. Every article has a serious purpose in it, and I, having the pleasure to be among the first to read all of them, have been asked by Dennis to write a preface to it and cannot refuse him. So I, despite my insufficient ability, have managed to write down the above words to finish my task.

CNOOD Yearbook (2018)

目录

1
施璐德序 2019
A Prologue to Our 2019 at CNOOD
Dennis Chi

10
砥砺自我
Self-Cultivation
Fay Lee

19
逗号、句号
From Retire to Restart
Alexander Tang

22
"解析变换"：施璐德，时刻准备着！
Prepare our CNOOD for Future by Analytical Transformation
Amir Tafti

29
系统研发二三事
Several Small Things in System Development
Nick Zhang & Ken Xu

34
见天地见众生见自己
Knowing, Doing, and Being
Tina Zhang

43
无惧岁月，笑看人生
Fear Not to Grow Old, and Enjoy Your Life with Smile
Tina Jiang

48
希望和意义
Hope and Meaning
Jack Sun

53
青未了
Unending Green
David Wang

59
心若不死，便有未来
Future Is There So Long As the Heart Lives On
Michael Wang

63
博观·约取·创作
See More, Take Less, and Write Creatively
Tony Liu

66
岁月与梦想
Times and Dream
Echo Lee

74
眼观日月，心入江河
See the Sun and Moon with Your Eyes, and Let Your Heart Merge into the Rivers
Echo Lee

84
人生的智慧
The Wisdom of Life
Johnson Shen

90
一次印象深刻的发运经历
An Impressive Experience of Shipment
David Lee

95
不合格报告管理系统开发
Non-Conformance Report Management System Development
Lay Tao

113
生活这件"小"事
Life Is But a "Small" Case
Jane Yan

122
曼德勒市市长耶伦博士到访施璐德EPC项目现场
Mandalay Mayor Dr. Ye Lwin Visit CNOOD EPC Project Site
Jackie Chen、Amanda Wu & Rocky Yuan

128
实习小结
Internship Summary
Zhou Chuang

134
春节小记
Spring Festival
Sissi Wu

137
我的父亲
My Father
Dennis Chi

142
母亲节 让我为你写首诗
It's Mother's Day; Let Me Write You a Poem
Tony Liu

145
小诗四首
Four Poems
Tony Liu

148
亚沙随笔
Random Writings About Asian-Pacific Business Schools Desert Challenge
Tony Liu

159
永远停不下的脚步
Footsteps That Would Never Stop
Billy Gu

163
CNOOD 代表团拜访罗马尼亚
——布加勒斯特市政府
CNOOD Delegates Visited Romania
—At the City Hall of Bucharest
CNOOD News

166
CNOOD 与上海财经大学经济学院签署战略合作协议
CNOOD Signed Strategic Cooperation Agreement with School of Economics, SUFE
CNOOD News

171
不忘初心
Stay True to Our Original Aspiration
CNOOD News

197
施璐德第一期国际项目经理资质认证 （IPMP）圆满结束
The 1st Training Session of IPMP at CNOOD Concluded with Success
CNOOD News

208
百舸争流，扬帆起航
A Hundred Boats Setting Sails in Speed Contest
CNOOD News

213
插花品香　邂逅最好的自己
Enjoy the Scent of Flowers, and Encounter the Best Self
CNOOD News

220
CNOOD 代表队参加静安职工三人篮球赛
CNOOD Teams Go In for Jing'an Staff-Member 3×3 Basketball Competition
CNOOD News

218
"美在静安　文明交通在身边"志愿者活动
"Beauty in Jing'an, Road Civility with Us": A Volunteer Service Campaign
CNOOD News

施璐德序 2019
——众志成城，为创建人人爱之、惜之、趋之的梦想之地，共同奋斗

A Prologue to Our 2019 at CNOOD
—United we stand. Let's work together to build a dreamland which everyone loves, cherishes and gravitates to.

■ Dennis Chi

先向各位同事、各位股东、各位董事、各位合伙人道歉。作为大家选出的董事长，没有做好工作，2017年和2018年没有分红。我们2016年股改，出发点是让大家一起分享公司成长收益。经过2013年到2016年接近4年的布局调整，EPC业务初具雏形，潜在项目层出不穷。尤其是CNOOD ENGINEERING SPA、罗马尼亚项目、VOPAK项目显示出极好的控制力、利润水平。即使保守预计，2017年分红不菲。当年给银行的工作汇报，我们也表达了这种积极的趋势。然而，由于项目股东和业主的变化，我们同时丢掉了这几个项目。这对当年的业绩产生了非常直接的影响，同时CNOOD ENGINEERING SPA的资本性支出，全部成为费用性支出。截至目前，我们的调整卓有成效，公司许多方面，体现明显。

First of all, I have to say sorry to all my colleagues, all our shareholders, all members of the Board of Directors, and all the partners of CNOOD. As the Chairman elected by all, I failed to do a good job and we did not pay dividends to shareholders in both 2017 and 2018. The equity structure reform in 2016 was aimed to enable all of us to share in the fruits of the company's growth. After a four-year adjustment during 2013-2016 we are now in the initial stage of EPC business with potential projects emerging in quick succession. CNOOD ENGINEERING SPA, the Romanian project and the VOPAK project in particular, have shown extremely good controllability and profitability. We foresaw a handsome pay of dividends in

　　Carol 曾经问我，Capricornio 项目是否可以重复。我的回答，当然可以。如同做大宗贸易商品，该行业有自身特点，不管谁做，情况会有所不同，但根本特点，没有谁可以改变。经过 2013 年到 2016 年接近 4 年的艰难但是始终如一的调整，以袁总最终成功加入施璐德为标志、以刘总成功拿下 Amador 项目为标志，以第一期施璐德 IPMP 培训及认证结束为标志，施璐德初步转型成功，成为可以承接石油、天然气、水处理、矿山、水电、风电、太

2017 according to conservative estimates. We also demonstrated this positive trend in our report to the bank. However, we lost these projects simultaneously because of changes in their shareholders and owners. This had immediate impact on the company's performance of that year, and the capital expenditures at CNOOD ENGINEERING SPA all became expenses. Up to now, our adjustment has been very successful as could be seen in many aspects.

　　Carol once asked me whether the Capricornio project was replicable. My reply was: "Of course it is!" The business of bulk trade is unique in its own way. Whoever does it will face different situations; however, its basic features won't be changed. After the hard but consistent adjustment during 2013 - 2016, and marked by Mr. Yuan's joining CNOOD, Mr. Liu's securing the Amador project and the conclusion of CNOOD's first session of

阳能,以及大中型基础设施项目的总包单位。该行业同样有其自身特点,这些特点是内生的,没有人可以任意改变。相信,施璐德的分红会越来越多。

非常抱歉,2018年10月的"capricornio 信任危机"。此次危机,比较充分暴露业务和财务之间缺乏信任,实质是对我的信任危机。智利合伙人 Mario 就说,Dennis 完全相信财务。最后,本次危机以非关联股东投票表决结束。作为董事长,我的确完全相信财务,相信他们为公司发展所做的种种努力,相信他们任劳任怨、勤勤恳恳的敬业精神,相信他们明明白白做事、清清楚楚做人的为人。

IPMP training and certification, CNOOD has been successful in its first stage of transformation and has become a general contractor in the fields including oil, gas, water treatment, mining, hydropower, wind power, solar energy, and large-and medium-size infrastructure projects. The business too is unique in its own way, with endogenous features which won't change easily. I believe that CNOOD will pay more and more dividends in the future.

I am so sorry for the "Capricornio Trust Crisis" in October 2018. It fully revealed the lack of mutual confidence between the business and finance departments. Fundamentally it was a trust crisis for me. Just as our Chilean partner Mario said, "Dennis completely believes the finance department." The crisis ended by a vote of non-related shareholders. As the Chairman, I do have complete belief in our finance department, in their willingness in work hard, diligence, conscientiousness and professional commitment, and in their high moral standards in doing things and dealing with others.

施璐德亚洲有限公司7位董事，是在公司发展过程中自然形成的，经过了种种考验，也依然继续在接受考验。所有董事，在公司发展过程中都做出了完全不可替代的贡献，不求名，不求利。所有董事，都在默默为公司发展，做着自己独特的贡献，不可或缺。正是这届董事带领大家的奋斗，给施璐德创造了发展机遇，奠定了飞跃的基石。大家的想法是一致的，是始终如一的：共同创造可持续发展的平台；大力培养年轻人；互相包容，互相成就，互相成全。我们不完美，但一直在完美的路上；我们有缺陷，但一直努力向前。追求蝇头小利的，不会有我们公司的气象；敢于透明的，不会有肮脏的内心。

公司的最高权力机构是股东大会，股东大会没有任期，终身制，继承制。公司其他所有机构都产生办法，有任期，有制约，有权限。任意股东，董事，监事，同事，都有对公司各机构，对公司所有人有监督权，都有抵制和制止伤害公司利益行为的义务和权力。譬如，董事长是大家选

The seven members of the Board of Directors at CNOOD have been chosen in the natural process of development. They have undergone various tests and are still being tested. With no personal interest in seeking fame or fortune, all of them have made irreplaceable contributions during CNOOD's development. They are silently making unique, indispensable contributions to the growth of the company. They have led us to strive and create opportunities for development, laying the foundation for future leap forward. We share the same consistent vision: to work together and create a platform for sustainable development; to put in great effort to nurture and train young people; to embrace the spirit of "Pristine Simplicity, Amorphous Unity, Reciprocal Constancy." We are not perfect, but are ever on the road toward perfection; we have defects, but are always doing our best to move forward. Anyone who seeks petty profits cannot be expected to be a true CNOODer, and anyone who doesn't fear transparency won't have a filthy heart.

At CNOOD, the General Meeting of Shareholders is the highest authority. Members of the Meeting have life-long tenures, while membership can be inherited. Every other organ of the company has prescribed rules of formation, terms of office, restrictions

出,如果其行为不当,失去任职资格,按照公司法,经临时董事会,或者临时股东大会,多数表决通过,即可罢免。大家都是股东,或者即将成为股东,这里是我们共同的家,伤害公司利益的行为,就是伤害大家的。不要做"老好人",看着歪风邪气,不闻不问,保持沉默,就是对公司的伤害。

and limit of authority. Any shareholder, any member of the Board of Directors and the Supervisory Board, or any colleague, has the right to supervise all the organs and owners of the company, and has the obligation and power to resist and prevent any behavior detrimental to the interests of the company. The Chairman, for instance, is elected by all members of the company. If he loses his eligibility for misconduct, he could be dismissed from office by a majority vote at an interim meeting of the Board of Directors or the General Meeting of Shareholders, according to the *Company Law of PRC*. Everyone is or will be a shareholder. CNOOD is the home of everyone and any behavior harmful to its interests is harmful to us all. Don't be a Mr. Please-all; you are doing harm to the company if you shut eyes to evil practice.

我们设立董事，建设董事会，成立股东大会，选举CEO，完善公司各职能机构，发展施璐德学会，为的就是去中心化，团结最广大的同事，发挥各位同事最大的能力，集中所有能够集中的智慧、能力，共同努力，建设一个人人爱之、惜之、趋之的梦想之地。

不管是什么职位，不管是什么职能机构，在施璐德，都是为所有同事服务的代表；所有权力，如果有，都是代表所有同事；所有股东，也是来源于所有同事，所有股东。

我们共同的家，需要积极向上的人，勇于上进的人，互相鼓励的人，努力学习的人，主动求知的人，乐于助人的人。不需要打击同事的人，诋毁他人的人，不求上进的人，无所事事的人，互相拆台的人，传播负能量的人。要敢于树立正气，打击邪气，为公司的成长创造一个良好的环境，为公司营造一个良好的氛围。努力奋斗，掩盖问题的，我们承受不起；无所作为，不求上进的，我们担当不起；领受工资，只干私活的，我们不欢迎；有负面情绪，不加节制的，我们不敢当。

By establishing the Board of Directors and the General Meeting of Shareholders, electing the CEO, perfecting the various functional departments and boosting the CNOOD Society, we aim to decentralize, to unite with the overwhelming majority of our colleagues and give full play to their abilities, to pool all the wisdoms and strengths, and, with concerted effort, to build a dreamland which everyone loves, cherishes and gravitates to.

At CNOOD, everyone is a representative to serve all colleagues, whatever title he has or whatever functional department he is in. All the authority, if any, represents and stems from all the colleagues and shareholders.

Our home needs people who are positive-minded, ambitious, mutual encouraging, fond of studying, eager to learn, and willing to help others. It doesn't need people who discourage colleagues, who slander others, who content themselves with the status quo, who fool about, who counteract each other's efforts, and who spread the negative energy. We should be brave enough to encourage the spirit of righteousness and check the unhealthy trends, creating a good environment for the growth of the company and a good atmosphere for the colleagues of CNOOD. We are not able to accept those who try hard but always cover up problems; we cannot afford to have those who are satisfied with the situation and

施璐德的文化，是"家文化"，"暖文化"，"爱文化"，是给所有施璐德人一个家，一个共同奋斗的地方，共同生活的地方，大家互相包容，互相成就，互相成全，但绝不藏污纳垢；一个温暖的家，大家互相关心，共同创造开心的海洋，但绝不容忍无所事事，无所作为；一个充满爱的家，不同的家庭，不同的种族，不同的地区和国家，不同的宗教，但绝不溺爱和纵容。

accomplish nothing; we do not welcome those who get paid only to do their personal business at office hours; and we dare not accept those who cannot control their negative sentiments.

The corporate culture of CNOOD is a culture of home, warmth and love. It offers a home to all CNOODers, a place where we work and live together with the spirit of "Pristine Simplicity, Amorphous Unity, Reciprocal Constancy", but is never a den of iniquity; it offers a warm home, with the motto "Caring Number of Others' Delightfulness, Creating New Ocean of Delightfulness", but never allows anyone to idle about; it is a home full of love, embracing different families, different races, different regions and nations, and different religions, but are never overindulgent.

2019，是承上启下的一年，新征程的开始。我们已经初步搭建起腾飞的平台，已经初步完善启航的队伍，需要所有同事的共同努力，兢兢业业，精益求精，精打细算，把每一个项目做成经典，在个人成长史上，在团队建设历史上，为所建设的国家和项目，留下浓墨重彩的伟大篇章。

做受尊敬的公司，做有尊严的公司。做受尊敬的人，做有尊严的人。苟日新，日日新，再日新。从来就没有什么岁月静好，只是有人在负重前行，让我们勇于担当，以无比的信心和勇气，共同携手，共同努力，为把施璐德建设成人人爱之、惜之、趋之的梦想之地而努力奋斗。

The year 2019 is a critical link between the past and the future; it marks the beginning of a new journey. We have preliminarily built up a platform for take-off, and have assembled a team ready to set sail. We need the joint effort of all our colleagues; we shall do our best and keep on improving, trying to make every project a classic case with meticulous planning and leaving brilliant chapters in our personal growth, in the history of our team, and in all the countries and projects we have worked for.

Be a respected company, a company with dignity. Be a respected person, a person with dignity. It is written in *The Great Learning*, "If you can one day renovate yourself, do so from day to day. Yea, let there be daily renovation." There would be no such things as "peaceful and good days"; we can have them only because someone is shouldering the burden for us. Let's assume the responsibilities and join hands with unparalleled confidence and courage, working together to build CNOOD into a dreamland which everyone loves, cherishes and gravitates to.

池勇海
Dennis Chi

池勇海，男，汉族，1970年生于湖北省仙桃市。武汉理工大学管理学硕士，硕士导师刘国新教授；复旦大学经济学博士，博士导师洪远朋教授。2008年创立施璐德亚洲有限公司，现担任施璐德亚洲有限公司董事长。

Dennis Chi, of Han nationality, was born in Xiantao, Hubei Province in 1970. He received his Master's degree in Management Science at Wuhan University of Technology, where he studied under Professor Liu Guoxin, and received his PhD in Economics at Fudan University, where he studied under Professor Hong Yuanpeng. Dennis is now Chairman of CNOOD ASIA LIMITED, which he founded in 2008.

砥砺自我

Self-Cultivation

■ Fay Lee

新年的到来，让人不由得便会与新的开始联系到一起。回顾2018，无疑对我们每个人来说都是充满意义与挑战的一年，我们取得的进步与成果，足以让我们每一个人都为之振奋。随着时间的逝去及那股兴奋的逐渐消退，当剥离了表面上的那一层糖衣，我发现，其实我们所走的路，比表面上更崎岖。最近我在思考这样一些问题："到底我们公司在市场中的价值是什么？""我们以什么赢得客户与市场？""我们的发展是可持续的吗？"

这些问题不仅关系到公司的发展，更关系到每一位CNOOD人的未来。我们把CNOOD作为承载梦想实现人生价值的地方，那么公司在市场中要有价值，我们每个人更要有个人价值。这个电脑随时能取

When the New Year is coming, I couldn't help associate it with a new beginning. As we look back, we find 2018 a year full of meaning and challenges for every one of us. We are all inspired by the progress and achievements we made in that year. With the passage of time and the gradual disappearing of excitement, the way we have travelled proves to be more rugged than it appeared when the sugar-coat has peeled off. I have recently been thinking about the following questions: "What on earth is the value of our company in the market?" "By what means can we win clients and the market?" "Are we developing on a sustainable basis?"

These questions concern not only the development of the company, but also the future of every CNOODer. We see CNOOD as a place where we realize our dreams and the value of life. While

代人类的时代，个人在公司中的价值又该如何去体现呢？

our company must have its value in the market, every one of us must also have personal value. In an era when human beings will easily be replaced by computers, how should we demonstrate our personal value in the company?

我先来谈一下公司价值，我们这几年转型发展 EPC，是因为我们早已看到传统的贸易模式，早就被阿里巴巴这样的电子平台给颠覆，电子平台上呈现了足够的商品信息，供应商可以通过电子平台直接把商品卖给需求方，然而现在却很难有一个电子平台可以做"工程总包"，按理说我们只要把足够的供应商信息呈现出来，也能给客户自助快捷的选择，我们为什么不建一个这样的电子平台呢？或许还能成为工程界的阿里巴巴，我们却将精力放在了 workbench 上，把 workbench 平台建设放在了工作流上，而非把重点放在信息发布上，那是因为，EPC 总包不仅仅是一个商品的转移的过程，或者是简单的"我给你盖一个厂房"，我们销售的产品各自差异很大，包含着满足客户不同层次的需求，需要各类资源的优化与整合。EPC 将设计

First of all, I would like to talk about the value of our company. In recent years we have been going through transformation and developing the EPC business, because we have already seen traditional patterns of trade be completely changed by e-commerce platforms such as Alibaba, on which sufficient information of products is shown and suppliers sell products directly to buyers. However, it is almost impossible for any e-commerce platform to become a "general contractor." Theoretically speaking, we can give our clients options to conveniently choose from on a self-service basis so long as we show enough information of suppliers on a platform. Then why didn't we build such a

院，供应商，施工队，融资渠道，物流等各类资源进行整合，而这些整合又是建立在人与人之间的交流之上，所以也包含着人文情感上的需求。客户做决策与选择的基础离不开人与人的交流，并非仅仅建立在商务信息交换上得出的结论。这正是我们努力带给客户的价值，也是我们在市场中的价值。

platform and become an Alibaba in the engineering industry? Instead of focusing on information release, we give more attention to Workbench, a platform which is built on workflow. That is because EPC means more than the process of transferring goods; it is far more complicated than "building a factory workshop for you." In fact, the products we sell are highly diversified and meet our clients' needs of different levels, calling for the optimization and integration of various resources. EPC is able to integrate these resources including designing institutes, suppliers, construction teams, financing channels and logistics. The integration is based on the person-to-person communication, and thus involves needs for human feelings. Person-to-person communication is indispensable to our clients' decision-and choice-making, which is not merely the result of exchange of business information. This is exactly what we try to bring to our clients, and is our value in the market.

延展开来讲我们要给需求方多方面、多层次的需求满足，多方面体现在我们对设计院，供应商，施工队，融资渠道，物流等各类资源的把控能力，我们是否做到了专业，是否做到了行业一流？多层次体现在我们在信息交流，方案呈现等工作上是否周到齐全，细致入微，沁人肺腑。做到这些我们需要有强大的专职工作人员，高素质的业务发展团队。到时我们就可以针对我们的工作团队进行信息发布，我们有一流的钢结构解决方案、港建解决方案、矿山解决方案、电力解决方案等，当我们销售的是我们一流的专业团队时我们就不可能被取代，当我们做到行业一流时就没人能取代我们。我们离这个目标还有距离，我们要多思考多学习，不盲目自信更不妄自菲薄，我们终将实现这一目标。

To elaborate on this issue, we are supposed to satisfy our clients' needs in multiple respects and at multiple levels. By "multiple respects" I refer to our controllability over designing institutes, suppliers, construction teams, financing channels and logistics. Are we professional enough? Are we among the first-rate companies of the industry? By "multiple levels" I refer to whether we are thoughtful, meticulous and well-received in information communication, presentation etc. In order to be so we must have strong, professional staff and high-quality business development teams. Then we are able to release information to our work teams, and will have first-class solutions for steel structures, port construction, mines and electric power. We cannot be replaced when we have the best professional sales teams. No one can replace us when we are among the first-rate companies of the industry. We still have a long way to go before reaching this goal. We have to think more and learn more. We should not be blindly self-confident, nor look down upon ourselves. We are bound to reach our goal.

再来谈谈个人价值，个人价值避不开话题是我们的工作在不久的将来会被人工智能替代吗？目前看到趋势是：那些重复性高，能被电脑识别归纳总结的工作，将首先被人工智能取代。比如：图像识别，声音识别，建立在特定样本数据范围内的工作。体现在具体的工作上就是：设备操控，特点问题解答，车辆驾驶，翻译等。随着传感器的发展，电脑计算能力的发展，人处理"物"的能力将逐渐处于劣势，电脑有着无可比拟的优势，这些物包括物理上的物质，也包括各类数据、单据、机械、电子设备等。人还能继续保持优势的方面是，在处理人与人之间的事务。试想一下，我们的 workbench 发展到一定程度，越来越智能地帮助我们的经营与决策，作为个人而言，我们是否依旧有能力在公司发展中保留有一席立足之地？绝不能使自己沦为简单重复劳动的工作者。当然，个人能力的培养也绝不是一蹴而就，要有足够的知识储备，要有丰富的工作经验，并且要在不断的自我革新中发展。

Next, I would like to talk about personal value. When it comes to personal value, there is one question that we must ask: "Will our jobs be replaced by artificial intelligence (AI)?" The trend, as we see now, is that highly repeatable jobs that can be identified and summarized by computers will be the first ones replaced by AI. These jobs include image recognition, sound recognition, and other jobs based on specific sample data, such as facilities control, answering specific questions, vehicle driving, interpretation, etc. With the development of sensors/transducers and the computing power of computers, the ability of human beings to deal with "things", i.e. physical matters

公司业务在往多元化发展，个人如何适应或者是引领这样的发展，便成为了当下我们每个人都需要去思考的问题。前面我们提到人与人之间的交流是我们工作中非常有价值的重点之一，也提到了人与人之间的事务是人工智能难以取代的，要别人喜欢与你交流，能与你建立顺畅良好的沟通，这对每个人的个人素养提出了极高的要求。个人素养由知识体系，思想格局，语言能力，学习能力多方因素决定，这也意味着我们需要去提升的点有很多。绝不能因为本身的良好基础便将自我提升搁置一旁，在快速变革的社会环境中，资历与经验将很快成为历史。

as well as data, documents, machines, electronic devices, etc., will gradually be at a huge disadvantage compared with computers. Human beings, however, can keep their advantage in dealing with person-to-person business. Just think about it: "Are we still able to secure a proper place in the company while our Workbench is rapidly developing to a certain extent and is helping us with business operation and decision-making in an increasingly intelligent manner?" Therefore, never become a worker engaged in simple, repeatable jobs. Admittedly, personal abilities cannot be developed overnight. One need to have enough accumulation of knowledge, rich working experience, and achieve personal growth with continuous self-innovation.

The company is developing toward business diversification. Every one of us must think about how to adapt to or lead such development. The person-to-person communication I mentioned above is one of the valuable highlights in our work; I also mentioned that it is hard to replace person-to-person business by AI. It requires high personal quality to make other people enjoy communicating with you and build smooth, effective communication. Personal quality is determined by multiple factors including your knowledge, way of thinking, language skills and learning ability, which means that there are many aspects to be improved. Never put aside self-improvement just because you have a

公司需要新鲜血液加盟，更需要我们的自我革新。在CNOOD，我们的每个人无论是在股东大会，在董事会，在项目团队中，都属决定性的力量，也是公司命运的核心驱动力。我们需要每个人找准自己的个人价值，公司会和你自己一起不遗余力的发展这份价值，无论是在公司内部，还是在大环境中我们每个人都需要保持竞争力，这场竞争不但关乎公司与公司，人与人，更关乎个人与人工智能。如果我们不认清时代，不能勇敢的面对现实，我们必将被时代淹没。

good grounding. In a fast-changing society, qualifications and experience will soon become history.

The company needs to bring in new blood, as much as it needs our self-innovation. At CNOOD, every one of us, whether a member of the General Meeting of Shareholders, the Board of Directors, or any project team, is a decisive power and a core driving force for the company's fortune. You are expected to find your personal value, and the company will spare no effort to help you develop it. Everyone must stay competitive whether within the company or in a larger environment. Competition exists not only between companies, individuals but also between individuals and AI. If we do not have a clear vision of the times and fail to face the reality

因此，个人能力的持续提升，将是我们未来重点关注的。希望我们所有的CNOOD人能够带着这样的紧迫感去思考，当你开始思考就已经的是领先了。刚过去2018年底我们开展了全员国际项目经理（IPMP）培训和认证，这只是我们针对CNOOD能够走向工程承包公司所推进的第一项人员培养措施。接下来，我们还将推进造价师，建造师，注册安全工程师等相关的人才培养和发展。当然，我们也将继续邀请专业人才加入CNOOD，进一步丰富我们的人才结构，优化整体业务能力，引领我们走向下一个里程碑。

bravely, we will inevitably be submerged by the tide.

In the future, therefore, we will pay more attention to the continuous improvement of personal abilities. I hope all CNOODers will think with a sense of urgency; when you begin to do so, you are already in a leading position. In the end of 2018, we carried out all-staff training and certification of International Project Manager Professional (IPMP). This is only the first step in training for building CNOOD into an EPC company. Next, we will launch training and development programs of Cost Engineer, Constructor, Certified Safety Engineer, etc. Meanwhile, we will continue to invite more professionals to join us, in order to further enrich our human resources

structure and optimize the overall business capabilities while marching toward our next milestone.

公司在全力为发展准备着，作为CNOOD人，我们需要能够独立思考与分析，找准自己的定位，培养正确的合作意识，并全力以赴。2019已经在春节的余热里拉开了帷幕，新的一年也是一个新的开始，也意味着新的蜕变。新的一年，我希望我们在CNOOD砥砺自我，心之所向，义无反顾！

The company is doing its best to prepare for future development. As CNOODers we need to be able to think and analyze independently, find our own positions, develop a right sense of cooperation, and go all out to achieve our goals. The year 2019 has begun in the lingering atmosphere of the Chinese New Year, which marks a new beginning and betokens a new metamorphism. In 2019, I hope that all of us will further cultivate ourselves at CNOOD and forge ahead toward what we are aiming without the least reservation.

李燕飞
Fay Lee

自省、学习，始终坚持自我进化；
做一个值得他人信任的人，不辜负每一次信任；
做一个让人觉得温暖的人，分享每一份正能量；
坚持理想与完美主义的信仰，
不忘主观与客观结合的分析，
执着于制订计划并付诸行动，
朝着所信仰的方向不断努力，
心之所向，义无反顾。

With soul-searching and learning, she persists in self-evolution.
Be a trustworthy person, and never betray any trust;
Be a warm person, and share every positive energy.
Hold fast to the faith in ideals and perfectionism;
Never forget analyzing things from both subjective and objective angles;
Persevere in making plans and put them into implementation;
Work tirelessly toward the direction of conviction.
Never turn back once heading for something the heart gravitates to.

逗号、句号

From Retire to Restart

■ Alexander Tang

有些人工作了几十年，辛勤劳累，就想着"年纪大了，该退休享福，不用工作了"。

有些人工作了一辈子，营营役役，但想着"老来生活无依，仍要继续工作，不敢退休"。

有些人工作年月不长，浑浑噩噩，也想着"最好得笔横财，马上退休享福，不用工作"。

"退休"，就是"不工作"吗？"不工作"就是"享福"吗？在我的字典里，答案都是否定的。

"退休"，是工作生涯的中途站，不是终点站；是人生诗篇的逗号，不是句号。

中途站停下来，可以换乘新车，奔往新的方向。逗号之后，可以转折新的风格，谱出新的诗意。

原来的工作退下来，可以休养生息，重新寻找新的工作路向。

在银行业工作了几十年，可以说经

Some people want to retire and rest, after decades of hard-working life.

Some people do not want to retire even they cannot work, because of living burden.

Some people always dream of fortune to make early retirement and not working.

Does "retirement" mean "not working", or does "not working" mean "happiness"? My answer is always NO.

Retirement is just a break but not an end of the working life. It is a stop but not the terminal of the life journey.

Taking a break, we can restart working with new challenge, new environment.

Taking a stop, we can continue our journey to new direction, new destination.

After decades of working in banking

验丰富，也可以说是有点厌倦了。年过半百，开始考虑——在到了银行的法定退休年龄后，离开了银行圈，我该做什么？能做什么？

是时候离开原来的江湖，跳进汪洋，感受一下新的风浪。

Cnood不只是一家企业，更是个平台，提供机会与每个参与者去发挥个人潜能，施展抱负。

加入施璐德，成为一个"年长的新丁"，希望能找到人生新的路向，谱出新的诗篇。

咱们一家人，互相支持，共同努力！

industry, it is time for me to think about… what shall I do, what can I do, after reaching the official retirement age?

CNOOD is not only an enterprise, it is also a platform that provides opportunities for each member to develop his/her talent and achieve the goal.

Joined CNOOD as a "new but old" member, wishing that I could write a new chapter for my own life.

Let's join hands to achieve our goals.

邓志强
Alexander Tang

邓志强先生于2017年7月加入施路德集团为合伙人。

邓先生为一资深银行家，拥有超过三十年在中国香港以及内地两地银行的实务经验。过去二十年，邓先生专注于亚洲地区客户的大宗商品融资业务，尤擅长各类结构性贸易融资产品的设计与风险监控。加入施路德之前，邓先生担任香港星展银行大宗商品业务主管达11年。

此外，邓先生也热衷于培育银行同业后进。工余为香港银行学会担任专业导师，主持各项培训课程。

Mr. Alexander Tang joined CNOOD Group as Partner in July 2017. Alexander is a senior banker with over 30 years' practical experience with banks. In the last 20 years he focused on financing commodity trade for clients in Asia and was a specialist in designing structured trade finance products and risk control. Before joining CNOOD, Alexander had been holding the position of Commodities Head at DBS Hong Kong for 11 years. Alexander is also enthusiastic in training young bankers and has been Associate Lecturer of Hong Kong Institute of Bankers for years in various topics.

"解析变换"：施璐德，时刻准备着！
Prepare our CNOOD for Future by Analytical Transformation

■ Amir Tafti

我迄今为止在政府部门和私营企业工作，拥有超过32年的专业经验。在这里，我想请各位思考这样一个主题：我们如何才能够让施璐德做好准备，有能力迎接将来的项目？

施璐德是一家年轻的企业，不仅从其创立的历史来看是这样，而且她的员工队伍也很年轻，所有人都在为了变得更完美而努力积累更多的知识和经验。我认为，人力资源激励最有效的途径就是自我提升，但这在很大程度上取决于工作环境。营造这样的工作环境，正是施璐德的职责所在。

当今时代，不论是施璐德还是全社会的年轻一代，都比以往任何时候更需要这样一种成长环境，它能够为相关的工作岗位照亮暗路。我们应当知道，一家企业就像一个小型社会，而每一个社会系统都需

As one person with more than 32 years special work experiences in both governmental & private sectors, I would like to pull you toward this subject that how we can prepare our CNOOD company for future projects?

CNOOD is a young company, not only according to date of establishment but also based on the working force that all of them are looking for more knowledge & more experiences to reach better perfection. I think the most powerful of human motivation is Self-Enhancement, but this highly depends on such kind of environment that you work in. So it is CNOOD's responsibility to prepare this environment for future.

In this era, the young generation of CNOOD & even of our society is more than ever in need of such kind of proper environment to grow up & can illuminate the dark paths of related jobs. We should

要设定所有成员共同追求的若干目标。

今天，世界上所有的公司都有明确的目标，并在团队政策的引导下，努力达成这些目标。当下，许多公司尝试在下述流程和方法的基础上整合相关项目：

（1）任何新方案的付诸实行，从项目规划到项目管理，全程均可通过团队协作的岗位体系轻松实现。

（2）任何一个项目均需要有团队协同的五个阶段：组建期、激荡期、规范期、执行期和休整期。

（3）团队发展过程中的问题包括：信任缺失、害怕冲突、投入度不足、标准过低、缺乏对结果的关注。

know that one company is exactly the same as one society, so every social system requires a number of objectives which are common between individuals.

Today all companies around the world have specific defined goals, & based on the teamwork policy work hard to reach the defined goals. Right now many companies try to involve the related projects based on the following procedure & methodology:

a) Implementation of any initiative from project planning & management can be facilitated through Teamwork jobs.

b) Each project needs the five stages of Team Synergy contain of: forming, storming, norming, performing & adjourning.

c) Problems in team development include inability to trust, fear of conflict, lack of commitment, low standards &

（4）可使用多种策略提高团队协作的有效性，包括：头脑风暴法、名义小组法、SWOT分析法、SBAR沟通模式。

尽管上述流程对于每一家企业都必不可少，但我们想要让施璐德做好准备迎接未来的项目，光有这些是不够的。事实上，"解析变换"必须建立在真实情景和逻辑思维的基础上。

现在，我们正面临着这样一个问题：如何才能够让施璐德做好准备，有能力迎接将来的项目？

最好的办法，是用"解析变换"对施璐德公司进行一番转型，其中，我们必须把重点放在四个关键模块上：

（1）数字战略（我们的业务将朝着哪个方向发展？）

（2）商业模式（战略方向怎样与我们现有的业务相匹配？）

（3）赋能因子（我们实现战略目标需要哪些手段？）

（4）组织协调（如何对变革加以管理，以实现最终目标？）

上述四个关键模块构成了"解析变换"的一个高阶体系。明确了这些之后，我们就着手进一步研究这些模块，形成"解析变换"的一套高阶方法。

inattention to results.

d) Multiple strategies maybe used to increase the effectiveness of teamwork & include the use of brainstorming, nominal group processes, SWOT analyses (Strengths, Weaknesses, Opportunities, & Threats), & use of SBAR (Situation, Background, Assessment, Recommendation) communication method.

Although these mentioned procedures are so necessary for each company, it is not enough that we can prepare our company for future projects, in fact Analytical Transformation must be based on the real situation & logical thinking.

Now we are facing this question that how we can prepare our CNOOD for future projects?

One of the best methods is that we Transform our company by Analytical Transformation that we must focus on four key blocks:

a) Digital Strategy (means where our business should be going?)

b) Business Model (means how that fits what our business does?)

c) Enablers (means what we need to get there?)

d) Orchestration (means how will we manage change to reach our goals & destination?)

These four key building blocks form a high-level system for analytical transformations. With these identified, we took a first step to exploring these further, forming a high-level method for

我们必须明白：任何一家公司的转型都是一个艰难的过程。有些公司取得了一些成效，但真正完成这一蜕变的却少之又少。公司的高管层没有面面俱到的战术手册可供遵循，甚至连任务清单也不存在。

在最初阶段，审慎的做法是向公司内外的其他人学习。这能为我们提供大量的经验；另一方面，我们能够借此研究转型带来的挑战，设计应对方案，并就如何转型以迎接未来的项目创建实用的工具。以下是关于这四个关键模块的几点说明：

1. 数字战略

作为数字战略的第一步，我们要解决三个关键问题：

（1）我们所在的行业正在向何处去？

（2）在未来，我们公司将扮演怎样一个角色？

（3）我们怎样才能创建一条前进的路径，在方向感和适应能力之间实现平衡？

我们还没有得到这些问题的所有答案，不过有一个引起施璐德共鸣的理念是：将"今日前推"和"未来后溯"结合起来。这样，每一项转型既包括那些在今天看来与捕捉商机息息相关的元素，也包括那些能够使公司驶入未来发展轨道的元素。

analytical transformations.

It is important that we know: transforming a company for future is tough. Many companies have had some success, but few have completed this metamorphosis. No comprehensive playbook, or even checklist, exists for executives to follow.

A prudent first step is to learn from others, both inside and outside our company. This brought us the huge amount of experiences, & on the other hand we can explore the challenges raised by transformation, design answers, and create practical tools on how to transform a company for future projects. & now some explanation around these four blocks:

A. Digital Strategy

As the first step, setting a digital strategy starts with confronting three key questions:

a) Where is my industry headed?

b) What will my company's role be in that future?

c) How can I create a path forward that balances a sense of direction with the ability to adapt along the way?

While we didn't have all the answers to those questions, one idea that resonated with CNOOD was to combine "today forward and future back", so every transformation must include elements that pursue business opportunities that are relevant today as well as those that put the organization on the path towards the future.

施璐德的发展路线图必须包括"今日前推"和"未来后溯"这两方面的元素。"今日前推"相关元素涌现自当前的项目,其中我们需要公司找出能改进当前业务的新方案。

这一双重性质的方法能够让我们具备清晰、均衡的视角,提升业务参与度,并促使高管层积极投身转型,力争取得成功。

2. 商业模式

我们必须明白,大多数转型仍然属于业务转型的范畴。这些转型必须能够为顾客创造真正的价值,能够产生更好的业绩,而不是"为技术而技术"。这些转型常常能带来顾客体验的升级、产品和服务的数字化、新的经济模式的诞生以及运营上的改善。

CNOOD's roadmap must include both today-forward and future-back elements. The today-forward components emerged from our current projects, where we asked the organization to identify initiatives to improve our current business.

This dual approach led to a clear, balanced vision, business engagement and a group of executives motivated for the transformation to succeed.

B. Business model

We should know that most transformations are still business transformations. They must drive real value for the customer and improved outcomes for the business, not merely install technology for technology's sake. These transformations typically result

3. 赋能因子

我们所做的一切，都需要对关键赋能因子作出改变，或是引入新的赋能因子，例如数据和分析方法、IT 系统、运营模式、人员以及企业文化。转型固然涉及技术层面，不过技术往往是相对容易做到位的。我们常常惊讶于转型的成功居然在如此大的程度上依赖于企业组织和文化，而要改变这些方面又是如此之难。我们最大的挑战，在于招聘新鲜血液，提升自身能力，并使企业文化朝着更具创新性和适应性的方向转变。

4. 组织协调

公司中很多人目前正在负责管理某一方面的转型，他们都清楚这一过程到底有多复杂。大多数项目一开始采取试点的形式，划拨专项资金，汇聚顶尖人才，在领导层强有力的支持下，开展小范围的试验。

在这方面，我们都看到了成功的案例。不过，要将这种试点进行下去并在全公司范围推广开来，仍然是一项艰巨的任务。在获取资金、改变多数员工（而不是仅仅 10 个人）的行为方式以及将转型融入遗留的 IT 系统等方面，我们仍然会遇到很多障碍。

总而言之，一旦我们弄清了转型需要哪些元素，我们就能够更详尽地讨论哪些

in shifts in the customer experience, digitalization of products and services, the emergence of new economic models, and advances in operations.

C. Enablers

All our journeys require changes to key enablers or the installation of new ones, data and analytics, IT systems, operating model, people and culture. While transformations are obviously about technology, technology often turns out to be relatively easy to get right. We were amazed at how much success really depends on organization and culture, and how difficult those can be changed. Our greatest challenges lie in hiring new talent, enhancing skills of our own, and shifting our culture to become more innovative and adaptable.

D. Orchestration

Many of us in the company are currently in charge of managing a transformation and realize how complicated the journey truly is. Most programs start with experimentation, a contained test with dedicated funding, top talent, and strong leadership support.

Here, we've all seen success. However, it remains a formidable task to then take that experiment and scale it throughout the enterprise. We run into obstacles around securing funding, changing the behavior of many people (not just 10), and integrating into legacy IT systems.

As conclusion, once we had articulated the elements required for our

领域是我们认为最具挑战性的，而哪些看起来在我们的掌控之中。我们将进一步深入探讨这些问题。

正如我在文章开头提到的，施璐德是一家年轻的企业，但拥有辉煌的未来。愿我们能够实现施璐德的转型，为将来的项目做好准备。

坚持学习，汲取经验，为我们辉煌的未来做好准备。

祝各位万事如意！祝施璐德蒸蒸日上！

transformation, we were able to discuss with some specificity which areas we find most challenging and which seem under control, & we will explore these topics in more depth.

As I mentioned at first, CNOOD is a young company, but with glorious future, hope so we can transform our CNOOD, will be ready for future projects.

Keep Learning, Collect the Experiences & ready for Glorious Future.

All the best wishes for you & our CNOOD.

Amir Tafti

我叫 Amir Tafti。飞行器工程本科毕业后，我在不同行业领域的政府部门和私营企业工作过，拥有超过 32 年的专业经验，尤其是在工业领域。回首往昔，有好几个理由让我相信自己是一个幸运的人。主要的一个理由是：我在同一个政府机构工作了 20 年，负责对我们国家不同的项目进行审计。我的第一份工作就是在政府部门，工作期间，我从一名普通的职员升为最高级别的经理。我学到了很多东西，并得以积累大量相关经验。此后，私营行业领域同样也为我提供了一个良好的、充满挑战的平台，使我能够成长为合格人才。

现在我已经 55 岁了，很荣幸成为施璐德团队的一员。我将尽我所能，把我的经验和知识传授给同事们，帮助营造一个更好的竞争环境。

I am Amir Tafti. With BS in Aircraft Engineering & more than 32 years of special work experiences both governmental & private in different sectors, especially industrial fields. When I take a look at to my past years, I find myself as one lucky person according some reasons. The main one for 20 years I worked in one special governmental office to responsible audit the different projects in my country, so I started my first & last job in government from common employee to top level manger, I learned a lot & can collected a huge related experiences. After that even in private sector is a good & challengeable platform for me to grow as qualified person.

Now in 55 years old, it is my pleasure to act as one CNOOD team & do my best to transfer my experiences & knowledge to my colleagues to create a better competitive environment.

系统研发二三事

Several Small Things in System Development

■ Nick Zhang & Ken Xu

2018 年我们秉承小步快跑、试错迭代的原则，自主研发的系统经历了 23 个大版本和 47 个小版本的升级，功能和交互得到不断完善。同时我们持续提升技术深度和产品思维，贡献开源社区。系统研发是枯燥的，需求又是鲜活的，经过思维的不断碰撞，整个过程变得生动和丰富。

有一次和同事聊天，被问到系统安全性怎么样，作为开发本能的说了一些安全方面的措施，如全站 HTTPS、两步验证、XSS 防护等。刚说完立马想到貌似有几个地方没有考虑 XSS 情况。随后回去看了一下代码，果然是用到的一个第三方的模板工具没有处理这种情况。一般这种情况都是分析一下第三方工具的代码直接帮忙

Adhering to the principle of "run fast in small steps, iterate by trial and error", we developed a system by ourselves in 2018. The functions and interactions of the system have been continuously improved while it went through 23 major versions and 47 minor ones. Meanwhile, we have been enhancing the technological level and the logic of the products on a sustained basis, making contributions to the open source community. R&D work is boring while the needs are fresh and vivid. The process becomes lively and enriched by constant brainstorming.

One day when I was having a chat with a colleague, I was asked how safe the system was. Out of the instinct as the developer of the system, I mentioned some of the security measures, including all-site HTTPS, two-step validation and XSS defense. It occurred to me immediately that there might be several

修复就可以了，但是看完代码后感觉这个工具设计的不太好，想了下立马决定自己重新设计一个工具，于是花了一个下午重新写了一个工具解决了这个问题。对于安全虽然我们会采用各种策略来保证，但我想说的是：没有绝对安全的系统，保护好个人信息才是最重要的。

places in the system where we had not taken into account the case of XSS. When I went back and had a check at it, I found as expected that a third-party template tool did not consider the case. A common practice would be analyzing the code of the third-party tool and just help fix the bug. After examining its code, I found that the tool was not well designed. I decided at once to design a new one by myself. I then spent a whole afternoon writing a new tool and solved the problem. Though we will use various strategies to guarantee the security of the system, what I want to say is: There is no system that is absolutely risk-free; the most important thing is to protect your own information carefully.

平时还会被问到系统能承载的用户数有多大，其实我们在设计系统时就考虑到了高并发的场景，尽量做到系统可以方便的进行水平扩展和垂直扩展。对于到底能承载多大用户量，其实我们是没有一个确定答案的，因为系统是一个不断演化的过程，用户少了单个机器就可以承载，用户多了可以通过简单的加机器来承载，要是用户再多了加机器是否有效、要如何加机器、业务要怎样拆分等就不确定了。因此只能说系统目前可以承载现有的用户量，至于能否到千万级、亿级要等到用户量真正达到那个级别的时候才会有说服力。

I am also often asked about the system's maximum load of users. In fact, we took into consideration the scenario of high concurrency when designing the system, making it as easy as possible to realize horizontal and vertical extension. As for the maximum load of users, actually we do not have a definite answer. It is because that the system is an ever evolving process: If we have only a few users, a single machine will be enough; if we have more users, more machines will be added; if we have even more users, it will be uncertain whether it is still effective to increase the number of machines, how they should be increased, and how the tasks should be divided, etc. There we can only say that the system is big enough to bear the current number of users. As for whether the system can reach a load of tens of millions or thousands of millions of users, it will more persuasive if we actually have so many users in the future.

还有一些同事比较好奇：我们系统容量有多大，每天上传很多文件会不会容量不够呀。一般我们会跟他们说我们是无限容量的，不存在容量不足的情况。但其实原因很简单我们的文件都存储在 CDN 上，而 CDN 本身就是用来解决资源的存储和分发问题的。目前我们的 CDN 并不是自建的而是采用第三方服务，除了成本方面的考虑外，主要还是因为现阶段还不需要且现阶段的技术储备还不够。

对于 Workbench 大家的第一印象是：它是公司内部一套项目管理系统用来把控项目的质量和进度。但其实这里涉及到两个误区，首先是内部还是外部，我们设计的初衷是没有内部和外部的区分的，我们把项目中涉及到的所有的人都认为是我们的用户，没有公司、地域的区分，大家都是通过互联网的方式来协作完成项目。另一个是系统还是平台，一般的系统指的是具有一定功能的软件集合，但是平台指的是一个环境，由一系列功能各异的系统组成。我们期望的是构建一个 EPC 行业的平台，同时这个平台会衍生出各种各样的服务，为所有 EPC 行业的从业者提供一个工作学习环境。

Other colleagues would be curious about the capacity of our system and whether the capacity is big enough if we upload too many documents. Usually my reply would be: "The system has an infinite capacity. There will never be such thing as 'insufficient space.'" The reason for this is quite simple: All our documents are saved in CDN, which is originally designed to address the problem of the storage and delivery of resources. Currently we do not build a CDN by ourselves but use the third-party service. This is not only because of costs consideration but also because of the unnecessity in the present stage and an insufficient technological reserve.

Your primary impression of Workbench would be: It is a project management system inside the company to control the quality and schedule of projects. However, there are two wrong ideas about this. First, inside or outside? We do not intend to distinguish between "inside" and "outside" in designing the system. We regard all the people involved in the projects as our users, no matter which company or region they are from. They work together via the Internet to accomplish a project. Second, a system or a platform? By "system" we generally refer to the collection of software with certain functions, while by "platform" is meant an environment comprising a number of systems with different functions. We expect to build a platform for the EPC industry, which would in turn

我们将日常的头脑风暴，先进的技术，秉承的管理理念融入到各个系统中。经过不断地打磨，它们的功能愈发完善，并服务于大家。当然，还有许多想法和功能未实现，也有许多困难需要克服，这都是我们工作的核心。未来的路任重而道远，让我们不忘初心，砥砺前行。

give birth to services of various types, providing an environment of working and learning for all the people in the EPC industry.

We ingrate daily brainstorming, cutting-edge technology and our managerial philosophy into all the systems. Their functions, through constant refinement, have been greatly improved and deliver better service to us all. Admittedly, there remain a lot of concepts and functions still to be realized and many difficulties to be overcome. These are at the core of our work. We shall shoulder heavy responsibilities in the future, stay true to the original aspiration and move forward through hardships.

张 牛 / Nick

张牛，技术合伙人，2015年加入施璐德，全面负责系统规划、研发和运营，一名奋斗中的程序员。

Nick, a technological partner who joined CNOOD in 2015 and a programmer who always works hard, is in charge of the overall planning, research and operation of system.

徐振震 / Ken

徐振震，技术合伙人，2015年加入施璐德，涉猎技术广泛，开源爱好者，代码洁癖重度患者。

Ken, a technological partner who joined CNOOD in 2015, has a wide range of interests in technologies. He is a lover of open source and a patient with severe "code mysophobia."

见天地见众生见自己

Knowing, Doing, and Being

■ Tina Zhang

电影《一代宗师》里，宫二说："习武之人有三个阶段，见自己，见天地，见众生，我见过自己，也算见过天地，可惜见不到众生，这条路我没走完，希望你能把它走下去。"这句话说了传统武术的大致修行次第。

我没习过武，从小学开始武侠小说倒是读了不少，以至于《九阴真经》、《大悲赋》、《灭绝十字刀》都烂熟于心。一直梦想自己成为一个大侠，各种招式出神入化，所以我拼命的学习，各种东西都涉猎，我希望能博览众家之长，最终能将手中的这把莲花剑耍得出神入化。在学习的过程觉得自己成绩已经很好了，我们从平凡的家庭起步，一点点积累，工能制图、文能写字、武能马拉松、娱能展歌喉，及至到更大的世界，才发现我所经年累月积累到二十多岁的东西，有些人可能十岁以前都会了，他们在向更广阔的世界行进。天地间，我辈仍是渺小一蜉蝣。但是这只小蜉蝣仍然在奋力地向前游动，既是日月

In the movie *The Grandmaster*, Gong Er says, "Mastery has three stages: Being, knowing, doing. I know myself. I've seen the world. Sadly, I can't pass on what I know. This is a road I won't see to the end. I hope you will." His words summarize the general sequence of cultivation in traditional martial arts.

I am not a practitioner of martial arts, but I have read so many kung fu novels ever since I attended elementary school that I can recite the *Jiuyin Zhenjing*, *Dabeifu* and *Miejue Shizidao* backwards. I used to dream of becoming a great man of chivalry, who has reached the height of perfection in all the techniques of fighting. So I learned hard and covered all kinds of stuff. I hoped that I could assimilate the strong points of all schools and would be able to use my Lotus Sword with superb perfection. I thought I did a good job in school studies. I was from an ordinary family. With gradual

精华造化、须得山川气概齐身。

记得刚工作的时候，进的是全球做水电 TOP2 的福伊特西门子。那时候，老板都是黄头发、总监都是笔挺的西装、秘书都是精致的妆容、客户都是全球能投公司、来往的不是政要便是大咖，交易的少则几亿多则几十亿的生意、出行都是飞机加五星级酒店……世界辽阔的气息铺面而来，一个象牙塔出来的黄毛丫头以为这就是天上人间。第一次在三峡大坝上感叹我们的鬼斧神工，第一次在外滩三号品红酒牛排，第一次在某大厦赏唐伯虎名画……工作的前几年一下子体验了半生的繁华。

accumulation, I became a person of versatile skills: graphics, writing, marathon, and singing. When I came to a wider world, however, I found that what I had accumulated for years until I was older than twenty, might already been mastered by others before ten. They are marching toward a much bigger world. People like me are but tiny mayfly in the vast universe. However, this tiny mayfly is still moving forward with all its might. We must display a majestic heroism since we are the creature by the essence of sun and moon.

When I began my career, I first joined Voith Siemens, a global top-2 hydro-power company where bosses were all blond-haired Westerners, directors were all in neat suits, secretaries were all with exquisite make-up, clients were all global energy investment companies, people we dealt with were either political VIPs or business tycoons, business transactions were valued by billions of dollars, and airplanes and five-star hotels were common for business trips...A vast world unfolds itself, and a rookie girl freshly coming out of the ivory tower thought it was heaven itself. I was amazed at the overwhelming scenery of the Three Gorges, tasted red wine and steak at "Three on the Bund," and enjoyed a painting by Tangyin (1470–1524, a master painter in the Ming Dynasty) at a so-and-so building—all for the first time in my life. It seemed that I had experienced the vanity of half a lifetime.

"你现在是为外国人在挣中国人的钱，何不到国企来为中国人挣外国人的钱呢。"在水利部农电所的邀请下，在外企工作近四年后，毅然踏进了有事业单位编制的国企，为其开拓国际市场，组建海外团队。第一次当水电工程项目经理的恐慌，要人没人，要钱没钱，要体系没体系，要积累没积累，周围全是没做过国外工程甚至说没有做过系统工程的新人，也是凭着一身孤胆和百折不屈的劲头向前冲，贼挡杀贼、佛挡杀佛，外企培养出来的谨小慎微、温婉优雅蜕变成一脸横肉、高喉大嗓、雷厉风行。我变成了供应商口中的"亚太那个女的"、土耳其工地现场工程师口中的"你们干嘛听TINA那个女人的，一个女人懂什么啊"、男同事口中的"难缠的主儿"……不讲人情、不按套路，活脱脱一个女霸王，最终我们的项目以欧洲最快的速度完成，彼时我如果做一个好人，做一个温柔优雅的女人，事情也许就会失控。项目执行无兄弟、办公做事无女人，如果您享受岁月静好，就一定有人替你砥砺前行。

"Now you are making money out of Chinese people for foreigners. Why not join us and make money out of foreigners for Chinese people?" On the invitation from the Institute for Rural Electrification, Ministry of Water Resources, I determinedly joined a SOE after I worked for a foreign-capital company for nearly four years. I helped it expand the global market and establish overseas teams. I still remember the fear and anxiety when I became the hydropower project manager for the first time. I lacked everything: people, money, system, accumulation. What I had around me there were new colleagues without the experience of overseas project or even system project. I ran ahead by all my guts and an unyielding zeal while overcoming all the obstacles getting in the way. The cautiousness and delicacy nurtured at the foreign-capital company were successfully transformed into tough looks, loud voice and the vigorous, speedy actions. I became "that lady from Asia Pacific" as mentioned by my suppliers. Turkish engineers at the project sites would say, "Why do you listen to Tina? What does a woman know?" Male colleagues would describe me as "a ticklish case." Unsympathetic and refusing to play the game in the conventional way, I was regarded as a virtual female tyrant. Eventually our project was accomplished at the fastest speed in Europe. In fact, things would have gone out of control if I chose to be a "nice" guy or a gentle,

于是，我们五六年时间干光了土耳其所有的项目，赶上了最好的时候，也为公司积累了不少的资金，风口上，我们这群猪也飞了起来。到处领奖、到处环游，商务部、水利部、科技部的领导出行跟着，国外的大使接待着，见了总统、见了部长、见了王子、见了将军，培训各第三世界国家部长、和各国参赞来往甚密、出行仪仗队般、言必被尊MADAM。那是另一番天地，是国家逐渐强大起来的风口、是率先走出去的风口、是背靠部委大树的风口……我为脚踩的这片大地骄傲，我以为接待了一下部长和政要，就真的成了代表中国形象的MADAM，就真的能有操盘的能力。

刚好赶上了中国的创业创新时代，不能被时代的脚步抛弃啊！七勾八兑又联合国外的同学一起豪情万丈地要把国外的汽

elegant lady at that time. There are no "brothers" in doing a project, and no "women" in the business. You could have the peaceful and good days only because someone else is shouldering the burden for you.

As a result, we finished all the projects available in Turkey. We had seen the good days, while making quite some money for the company. As a saying goes, "Even a pig can fly if it can find a place in the eye of a storm." Traveling around the world, I was receiving prizes here and there. I was with the "big potatoes" of the Ministry of Commerce, the Ministry of Water Resources and the Ministry of Science and Technology on business trips; I was meeting with ambassadors from other countries; I was paying official calls on presidents, ministers, princes and generals; I was training ministers from Third-World countries; I was having close relations with commercial counselors from various countries; I was welcomed by "guard of honor" and addressed as "Madam." That was a different world. I found a place for myself by being among the first ones to "go international" with strong backing of the ministries when my country was becoming stronger. I was proud of the earth I set my feet on. I really thought I was the "madam" who, representing the image of China, had the power to control things.

"I should not," I said to myself, "be cast aside by the times in an era of widespread entrepreneurship and

车变速箱技术、核电后处理技术引进中国，各种混迹投资圈，听大佬们讲述各种投资故事，有一夜暴富的、有破产跳楼的、有香艳光怪的。马云的互联网咱们赶不上，模式创新咱们技术怪也不喜欢，但是还是受到技术成功的校友企业海康威视、高德红外、利亚德的影响，想要借用资本的力量，在机械或电力上有一些新东西能够一展抱负。

记得在见一个科技类投资人的时候，给他讲我们的技术和市场，他仔细看过后幽幽地说："你们这些项目需要时间的打磨、技术的积累，没有十年的磨砺，不可能成。"当时那个心炸裂的感觉，我现在都还记得，十年啊，青葱都要磨成老葱了。也许就是听了这个投资人的十年论，我的合作伙伴选择了和我分道扬镳。犹记得他的借口："如果你十年前在我一无所有时遇到我，彼时年少，互相没有依靠，我们可以一起携手十年创造辉煌，可是现在不一样了，我已经有了一些东西。"其实我想给那个伙伴说，每个时期遇到的伙

innovation." Through various connections I collaborated with my classmates abroad who were full of heroic spirit and enthusiasm, trying to introduce automobile transmission technology and nuclear re-processing technology to China. I mixed in with investors of various industries, listening to the stories told by the industrial tycoons: stories about someone getting rich overnight, those about someone going bankrupt and committing suicide by jumping off a building, or those amorous and grotesque...We could not hope to catch up with Jack Ma in the field of Internet, nor were we "tech geeks" fond of innovation in business models. Inspired by technologically successful companies founded by our schoolmates including Hikvision, Guide Infrared and Leyard, however, we still wished, by using the force of capital, to have something new in the fields of mechanics or electric power to achieve our ambitions.

As I recall it, when I met with an investor in the science and technology area and explained to him our technology and market, he said in a faint voice, "You need time for refining these projects and accumulating technology. You will achieve nothing unless you put in ten years of hard work." I remember vividly the feeling as if my heart had exploded. Ten years! By then we will all be presented with "a crown of glory." It was probable that my partner chose to part company with me because he agreed with this

伴都是那个时期和你旗鼓相当或者说你到了一定层次后才会遇到的人，糟糠妻是糟糠时遇到的，公主是功成名就时遇到的，马云刚开始只能遇到十八罗汉、有了一定基础时才有机会遇到孙正义和蔡崇信，每个时期的人都是那个时期你可以匹配的人，每个时期的人都很重要。众生皆是！

那段时期我很迷茫，不知道该坚持自己还是随波逐流，直到遇到Dennis，遇到CNOOD，那是他乡遇故知、久旱逢甘霖、高山觅知音等等的喜悦，Dennis说得很多话都是我想说的，Dennis想做的事也是我想做的，Dennis开坛授课所讲的思想体系就是我经常胡思乱想都想过的，苦于自己没有系统的思想体系构建能力，所以不能完整构建起来……从心出发、坚持做自己、跟随内心、内圣外王等等，都是我原来想过，但是没有去坚持的。

theory of "ten years." His pretext was as follows: "If you had met me ten years ago when I had nothing at all and when we were both young and independent, we would have been able to work together and create a period of glory lasting for ten years. But things are different now; I have already had something." What I wanted to say to my partner was: "The partner you meet at a certain time is always the one with equal abilities or the one you will not encounter until you have achieved a certain level. A man will meet his wife who shares his bad fortune only when he is having hard days, and he will meet a princess only when he has achieved both success and fame. In his early stage of entrepreneurship, Jack Ma could only meet the 'Eighteen Arhats.' It was at the stage when he had achieved something that he was able to meet Masayoshi Son and Joseph Tsai. People you meet in every stage of life are those well matched to you at that specific time. And they are all important to you. This is true for everyone!"

I was quite confused at that time, not sure whether I should stick to being myself or drift with the tide, until I met Dennis and CNOOD. That was a joyous event like "meeting an old acquaintance in an alien land, having sweet rain after a long drought, or finding a bosom friend who appreciates my talent." Many of the remarks by Dennis are exactly what I want to say, the things he plans to do are exactly what I want to do, and the system

Dennis 是一个很好的导师，他开启了我的天眼，让我看到了我自己，让我知道我从哪里来，要到哪里去，我要坚持什么，我要成为什么样的人，我能做什么，我不能做什么，让我知道悟道何时都不晚，让我知道坚持积累的力量，世界上没有一蹴而就的事情，你想要到达的境界必是经年累月的积累水滴石穿的力量。

当然，在一些操作方法和执行层面的问题，我和 DENNIS 的看法不一样，他也没有教过我很多操作方面的手法，也曾苦恼和烦闷，但是没有很多纠结，此刻我内心很坚定，没有怀疑过他，也没有怀疑过自己。就算他也会冒出一些出乎我意料的想法，也会听到一些言论，我仍然坚信他是我见过最好的思想 Leader，就像《阿甘正传》里的阿甘一样，有一种人，他是天生的思想强大的 Leader，他只负责向前不停地跑，跋山涉水、风雨无阻，跟随的人自然跟随，不跑的自然掉队。这种力量，开启了我思想的天眼。

of thoughts he explains in his lectures is exactly what I once imagined in wild fancies. I was not able to build a system as he did because of my inability in systematic construction...I used to think over all the following ideas, and yet failed to adhere to them: "Start from the heart." "Stick to being yourself." "Follow the heart." "Gain a learning both sound in theory and practice."

Dennis is a great teacher. He has opened my eyes, enabling me to see myself and to know where I am from, where I am going, what I shall stick to, what kind of person I want to be, what I could do and what I could not do. He has made me aware that it is never too late to achieve enlightenment. He has made me understand the power of perseverance: Rome is not built in a day; if you want to enter a new world, it must be the result of many years' effort like "dripping water wearing through a rock."

Dennis and I sometimes have different opinions as regards operational methods and the way of implementation. He did not teach me much about operation-level methods. I experienced depression and vexation, but did not have much mental struggling. At this very moment I am determined at the bottom of my heart, never doubting him or myself. I firmly believe that he is the best leader of thinking I have ever seen even if sometimes he will suddenly produce unexpected ideas or even if I will hear some unfavorable remarks about him.

在他的影响下，我逐渐沉下心来认识到我自己，我既不会自大以为自己是天上闪耀的星，也不会自卑认为自己是低如尘埃的土，我知道哪些是平台给我的力量，哪些是我自己积累的财富，我认清自己的优势和劣势。不急不躁，缓缓而来，无惧无怕，无怨无悔。我不再趋求他人的认同，我开始自己认同自己；我不再听阿谀奉承，我知道自己的段数和斤两；我不怕打击和诬陷，我知道此心光明夫复何言。

"古今之成大事业、大学问者，必经过三种之境界。'昨夜西风凋碧树，独上高楼，望尽天涯路。'此第一境也。'衣带渐宽终不悔，为伊消得人憔悴。'此第二境也。'众里寻他千百度，回头蓦见，那人正在灯火阑珊处。'此第三境也！"也许这正是见天地、见众生、见自己最好的注释，现在便依然是见山是山，见水是水，见自己是自己。

Just like the hero in Forrest Gump, he is born to be a leader with strong thinking ability, who trudges across mountains and water, stopped by neither wind nor rain. People who choose to follow him will naturally do so, and those who choose not to run will naturally drop behind. This power opens my eyes.

Inspired by him, I begin to calm down to know myself. I am neither so arrogant as to consider myself a sparkling star in the sky nor so self-abased as to consider myself a dust on the ground. I am able to distinguish between the strength given by the platform from the assets I have accumulated by myself. I have a good understanding of my advantages and disadvantages. I show great patience, bide my time, fear nothing and regret about nothing. I no longer seek the acceptance of others, but rather begin to be accepted by myself. I no longer listen to the flattering words since I know my own level and rank. I do not fear being discouraged or framed up. What else shall I say since I know my heart is full of brightness?

Anyone who has accomplished a great undertaking or made great achievement in learning must have entered three realms one by one. 'Last night the western breeze/Blow withered leaves off trees. / I mount the tower high/ And strain my longing eye.' This is the first realm. 'I find my gown too large, but I will not regret; / It's worthwhile growing languid for her.' This is the second realm. 'I look for her in vain. When all at once I turn my head, /I find her there where lantern light is dimly shed.' This is the third realm.

This remark, made by a great Chinese scholar, might be the best annotation on "knowing, doing, and being." Now, I remain in a state of "seeing a mountain where there is a mountain, seeing a river where there is a river, and seeing myself where there is myself."

Keep silent, and you'll see yourself and the beautiful scenery.

不言不语，见自己，便是好风景！

张丽萍
Tina Zhang

毕业于华中科技大学机械学院，非典型性工科女，从事能源电力行业十余年，在外企国企民企间自由切换。在做事中修行，在为人中修心，世上所有不过在于用心之深，用心之细，用心之诚。

As an atypical female engineer who graduated from School of Mechanical Science & Engineering, Huazhong University of Science and Technology, Tina Zhang has been in the energy and power industry for over a decade, switching without difficulty between foreign companies, state-owned enterprises and private firms. Her motto: The self-cultivation lies in the way you do things and conduct yourself in society. All things in the world depend only on deep, meticulous and sincere devotion of attention.

无惧岁月，笑看人生

Fear Not to Grow Old, and Enjoy Your Life with Smile

■ Tina Jiang

时光匆匆，岁月悠悠，转眼间，2018年就到了年终。2018年发生了很多意料之中和意料之外的事情。意料之中的事还好，尽在把控之中。碰到意料之外的事尽管会措手不及，但也有好处，它能警醒我们世事未必如愿，也能激励我们行动刻不容缓。有些意外敦促我们改变现状，有些意外则表明我们期待的改变已经在发生。在年初的时候，FAY分别找了我和我们的部门成员沟通交流，随着公司业务模式的调整，我们不能一直沉溺于自己的那块小天地，躺在过去的成就上。作为支持部门，我们要走出去，要深度参与，要和业务部门一起并肩奋斗，给予业务部门更多更专业的支持。

With the quick passage of time the year 2018 is now coming to its end before we notice it. Many expected and unexpected things happened in 2018. While we had complete control over expected things and were OK with them, we sometimes were caught unprepared by unexpected things. However, there is yet something good about un unexpected thing: It reminds us that life is not a bed of roses, and that we shall brook no delay in action. Sometime accidents urge us to make changes in the current situation; others indicate that the changes we have longed for have been taking place. At the beginning of the year, Fay communicated with me and other members in my department respectively. In fact, with the adjustments in the business model of CNOOD, we cannot afford to confine ourselves in our own old, small world and rest on the laurels. As a supporting

其实作为一名老员工，我很庆幸自己来到 CNOOD 这个大家庭，身边有一群活力充沛的小伙伴，志同道合的朋友、家人也时刻让我感受到家的温暖。工作上让我有了一片新天地，不再像过去一样整天埋在信用证和单据堆里，做出来的单据可以论斤来算，日复一日、毫无激情的工作，一眼望到头的职业生涯，其实也挺没意思的。现在我有机会接触到新的领域，学习更多新的知识，工作内容也更有挑战性和新鲜感。在变着花样的挑战中提高能力突破自己的瓶颈，一心寻求自身的进步，不断打磨自己。

其实在 2018 年有段时间也非常焦虑，焦虑工作的压力，焦虑孩子的学习、家里老人的身体状况……害怕失败，害怕批评，害怕失去……等等。后来跟一个好友聊天，她说，其实现在像你这样情况的人很多，每天活在焦虑中，而这种焦虑主要是在于自己总是在做加法，要更多，越要越觉得自己缺失；不敢停下来，每天都在追着时间的脚步跑，逼着自己往前。其实不妨放慢自己的节奏，善待自己，放松身心。忙时就做到专注，闲下来时，享受当下，享受生活中小小的幸福。人生不如意十之八九，但是我们都在努力地活着。在最苦的时候要乐观，在最难的时候要坚

department, we must go out for in-depth involvement. We should fight side by side with business departments and give them much more professional support.

As a veteran of the company, I feel lucky to have been to the CNOOD family, where I have many energetic colleagues around me. I can always feel the warmth of a sweet home because of the like-mined friends and family members. Instead of immersing myself in piles of LCs and documents, which could be weighed by kilogram, I am now able to embrace a new world. Insipid daily work and a career with nothing new to expect have no attraction for me at all. Now I have the chance to get into new areas and learn more new things, doing jobs with more challenges and novelty. Through various challenges I enhance my abilities and break the bottleneck in my career, earnestly seeking personal progress and continued refinements.

As a matter of fact, I felt great anxiety during a period in 2018. I was anxious about the pressure of work, the school record of my kid, and the health conditions of my parents... I was afraid to fail, to receive criticism, or to lose something important... Later, a good friend of mine said in a chat with me, "There are many people who are exactly like you, living in constant anxiety. They are experiencing anxiety because they always 'add things up' and want something more. The more they want, the stronger is their feeling of lacking

持。等回过头看所经历的艰难的日子的时候，以往走的每一步都是授予未来的勋章。与其抱憾和不舍，不如放过自己，试着让自己过得坦然充实，好好生活，努力赚钱，摒弃不必要的负担，对自己负责。

something. They dare not have a pause and race against time every day, forcing themselves to go ahead. However, it will do no harm to slow down, be kind to yourself and just relax. Concentrate on your work when busy; enjoy the present moment and the small happiness in life at your leisure. As the saying goes, 'If wishes were horses, beggars would ride.' But we still try to live a worthy life. Be optimistic in the hardest times and hold on under the most adverse circumstances. When we look back on the tough days we once had, we would see every step as

新的一年，放下过去，让心归零。在过去的一年里，对于所收获的，满怀感激，对于所失去的，也不要太过遗憾；认认真真的道别，再继续前行。很多事情，我们无法控制，便只能控制自己。别让过去的阴霾，影响了未来的灿烂。愿我们都能用心对待身边的人，用心把该做的事做好，按照内心所想的去生活，努力成为更好的自己。

a medal for the future. Instead of being regretful and reluctant to part, you had better let youself off and try to have a full, composed life. Live, work hard and make more money. Get rid of unnecessary burdens. Be responsible for yourself."

In the coming new year, let us forget old things and clear our mind. Be grateful for what we get in the past year, and yet don't feel too sorry for what we lose. Say goodbye seriously to the past before moving forward. We cannot control many things; what we can do is to control ourselves. Never let shadows in the past days impact the splendor of future. May we be able to treat people with a genuine heart, do a good job in what we should do, live according to our inner principles, and endeavor to be a better person.

姜 洁
Tina Jiang

作为一个5岁小女孩的妈妈，在陪伴孩子的过程中发现不只是孩子需要成长，自己也需要不断成长，只有自己变得更好，才有能力把孩子教育得越来越好。慢慢地，你会在孩子成长的过程中，发现TA的身上透漏着你的气质。你的动作，你的话语，甚至是你的脾气都在影响着TA。因为你努力的样子，孩子也看得到。

As the Mom of a five-year-old little girl, Tina Jiang has realized, while being with the child, that not only the child but also herself need to grow constantly. You will be able to educate your child and make him/her become better and better only if you become better yourself. Gradually you will find your temperament reflected in your child while he/she is growing. A child is influenced by your gestures, speeches or even your temper. After all, the way you make effort is also seen by your child.

希望和意义

Hope and Meaning

■ Jack Sun

一、前言

2018年8月底给CNOOD做了一次培训之后，Heather邀请我投稿CNOOD的公众号，同时会收编到《施璐德年鉴2018》中，不限主题和字数。我答应三周完成，但时间很快流逝，却仍未找到灵感。也不想匆匆堆砌，就此交差。下午会议之后，随手翻了翻CNOOD刚刚快递给我的中秋礼物——《施璐德年鉴2017》，感受着其中各种人和事所散发的激情和文化。遂顺势写下了我对CNOOD的认知，并且命名主题为希望和意义。

1. Foreword

When I finished a training course for CNOOD at the end of August, 2018, Heather asked me whether I could write an article for their official WeChat account, with no requirements as regards the topic or the length of it. I promised to finish it within three weeks; however, as time went by quickly, I could not find the inspiration. I did not want to write it in a rash just to finish my task. After the meeting this afternoon, I randomly paged through the *CNOOD Yearbook 2017*, a freshly arrived Moon Festival gift from CNOOD. While feeling the passion and corporate culture reflected by people and things in the *Yearbook*, I am now writing down what I understand about CNOOD, the theme of which I would like to name as "Hope and Meaning."

二、希望和意义

克拉克在他的科幻小说《最后一个地球人》中很好的阐述了这两个要素，他们分别是希望和意义。文中提到希望和意义是我们能够对抗巨大的困难和挑战，哪怕是死亡的最好信仰。

希望，就是让人们能够预知到未来。世上绝大多数恐惧来源于对未来的不确定性，并且恐惧的蔓延最终会带来灾难性的打击。给人们以未来，告知他完成现有的任务或活动后会获得什么样的回报、效果或目的，这样可以大大削弱未知性恐惧，是人们能够更坚定的有信心的克服人生或工作一个个困难，一步步走下去。

2. Hope and Meaning

In his science fiction novel *Childhood's End*, Arthur C. Clarke well explained the two elements: hope and meaning. In the novel he wrote that these two elements are our best conviction by which we are able to confront huge difficulties and challenges–even death.

HOPE is what enables people to see the future. Most of our fear comes from the uncertainty about the future, and the spreading fear will eventually bring about catastrophic hits. By giving people a future, and telling them what returns, effects or objectives they could achieve when they accomplish the current mission, we are able to greatly reduce their fear to uncertainty and enable them to overcome the difficulties in their life or work with determination and confidence.

意义，就是指所做的事有价值，能够给个人、家庭、企业、社会带来好处。有人会说：活得有价值，实现人生理想，有钱又有名，就是人生最大的意义；也有人说：过的开心，自由自在，就是活着的意义。还有人说：用一生或者半生，只做一件有意义的事，并将它做到极致，才是最大的意义。《士兵突击》中许三多说过"有意义就是要好好活，好好活着就是做有意义的事"。每个人的意义不同，但是最重要的是要有意义，让一件事有意义了，就能够让人产生强大的动力和支撑力，使其完成任务坚持走下去并取得成功。

MEANING is what gives value to the things we do, benefitting ourselves, our families, our company and the society. Some would say, "We achieve the greatest meaning of life when we have realized our value and dreams with fame and fortune." Others say, "The meaning of being alive lies in the happiness and freedom." And still there are people who will say, "If you do only one thing with your lifetime or half your lifetime, and bring it to the uttermost supremacy, you achieve the greatest meaning of life." In the TV drama *Soldiers Sortie*, Xu Sanduo has a well-known saying, "To do meaningful things is to live well, and to live well is to do meaningful things." Different people have different meanings; however, the most important thing is to have it anyway. If something becomes meaningful to you, it will generate powerful motive force and inspire you to hold on until success is achieved.

三、CNOOD 在前行

我眼中的 CNOOD 就是一家能给人以希望和意义的具有一丝传奇色彩的公司。池总规划的 CNOOD 制度，使上升没有限制，发展没有瓶颈，人人都有连续上升空间，把平凡的人变作不平凡。这样的制度给所有员工带来了希望；同时 CNOOD 一直秉承互相包容，互相成全，互相成就这三项双赢必备的理念，与战略合作伙伴优势互补，团队效应最大化发展，并且不忘社会责任。这样的运营理念给所有员工带来了意义。

3. CNOOD Is Forging Ahead

In my eyes, CNOOD is a legendary company that is able to give people hope and meaning. The CNOOD institution planned by Dennis sets no limit to promotion and development, and every person has the room for continued development, turning ordinary people into extraordinary ones. Such an institution brings hope to everyone. In the meanwhile, CNOOD has adhered to the philosophy of "Pristine Simplicity, Amorphous Unity, Reciprocal Constancy"

which is essential to win-win situation. Complimentary to its strategic cooperative partners, it maximizes the team synergy, without forgetting its social responsibility. Such a business concept brings hope to all people in CNOOD.

每每跟同事、朋友、客户等谈起CNOOD这家公司，我都心怀敬意。因为CNOOD在池总、Fay总的带领下，招募了大量的非常出色的优秀人才，组建了一个强大的团队。在CNOOD文化的推动下，可以完成很多不可能完成的任务。他们坚持着创新，怀揣着梦想，充满了热情，在制造业整体低迷的大趋势下，在走向EPC工程公司的道路上，一直闪着耀眼的光，值得敬畏！

I am always filled with admiration every time I talk about CNOOD with my colleagues, friends or clients. Led by Dennis and Fay, CNOOD has accumulated many outstanding talents and has formed a strong team. Inspired by the CNOOD culture, they have completed many missions impossible. Persevering in innovation and with dreams and enthusiasm, they have been

最后祝 CNOOD 越来越好，给更多的人带来希望和意义，创造更多奇迹！

shining brightly along the path toward an EPC company amid the overall stagnancy in manufacturing. They certainly deserve respect.

Finally, I would like to wish CNOOD a better future. I wish it to bring hope and meaning to more people with more miracles.

NOV Tuboscope Jack 写于 2018 年 9 月 18 号

Jack
NOV Tuboscope
September 18, 2018

孙 波
Jack Sun

孙波，国民油井 NOV Tuboscope 运营经理，交大安泰 MBA，持有 CWI，PMP，CSCP 等证书。先后就职上海振华重工，山特维克，国民油井等公司，专注国际化项目在中国运营，为中国制造业发展而努力！

Jack Sun, CWI, PMP, CSCP, is an Operations Manager of NOV Tuboscope. He received his MBA from Antai College of Economics & Management, Shanghai Jiao Tong University. Before joining NOV Tuboscope, he worked for Shanghai Zhenhua Heavy Industries Co., Ltd. (ZPMC), Sandvik, etc. Focusing on the operation of international projects in China, he works for the development of China's manufacturing industries.

青未了

Unending Green

■ David Wang

你站在桥上看风景，
看风景的人在楼上看你。
明月装饰了你的窗子，
你装饰了别人的梦。
——卞之琳《断章》

结识施璐德公司，是一种缘分，也是一种注定。缘分让莱茵和施璐德相识于2011年的金秋，而命运注定相互守望。到2019年的初春，我们之间的故事已经跨过七年之多，而且还将继续下去，装饰彼此的梦。

作为莱茵公司最早一批与CNOOD接触的"元老"，我的内心也是感慨万分。这七年多中，去过施璐德公司无数次，从环球世界大厦的9楼、10楼到越商大厦的

When you watch the scenery from the bridge,
The sightseer watches you from the balcony.
The bright moon adorns your window,
While you adorn another's dream.
——Bian Zhilin, "Fragment"

It was a destiny and fate to get to know CNOOD. Destiny has brought TÜV Rheinland and CNOOD to each other in the autumn of 2011, and fate has led the mutually supporting relationship all the way. Till to the early spring of 2019, we have a story lasting for more than seven years and will continue to adorn each other's dreams.

As a veteran from TÜV Rheinland to get in touch with CNOOD, I am filled with a myriad of emotions. I have been to CNOOD many times, with her address

8楼，见证了施璐德公司从几十人扩大到几百人，见证了一个个成功项目的完成，从主营业务单一的贸易公司转型成多元化多领域的国际EPC公司，无疑在我的心目中，施璐德公司是一家非常成功的公司。

changing from the 9th and 10th Floor of Universal Mansion to the 8th Floor of Yueshang Plaza. I have witnessed her growth from a company with scores of employees to a big one with hundreds of members, her success in completing one project after another, and her metamorphosis from a single-business trade firm into a highly-diversified international EPC company engaged in multiple fields. CNOOD, to my mind, is without doubt a very successful company.

在众人眼中，成功永远是一个极具魅力的词语，然而却鲜有人去细细地深思成功到底是靠什么来取得的？有人说，成功是凭借好的运气而获得的；也有人说，成功是靠自己的勤奋和努力而换回的；还有人说，成功是凭借不断的累积和坚持而获得的……其实，种种对成功的定义，我们都不可否认和拒绝，但值得肯定的一点是，成功 = 好的团队 + 好的机制 + 勤奋努力 + 不断坚持。

施璐德公司的"共创、共享、共治"的合伙人机制，成为她的事业成功的上层建筑规划。而每一个施璐德人身上充满的热情和激情，充满了爱，充满了执着和追求完美的品质，"互相包容，互相成全，互相成就"的企业发展文化理念，为这所房子添砖加瓦，构建起了施璐德这个美好的大家庭。

在与施璐德合作的项目中，我们双方项目组成员有过争吵，起过矛盾，但出现问题时双方都不会相互推脱责任，而是一起想办法共同去解决问题。这是因为我们都有共同的一个目标，做好每一个项目，把控好产品质量，将中国制造的每一件产品都打造成精品，达到国际一流水平。这也是为什么在很多施璐德的项目中，对于质量的要求都是高于行业和产品标准，因为符合标准只是我们的最低底线，我们的最高是追求卓越。

In the eyes of all people, "successful" is always a word with its own charm. However, few would begin to think about how the success is achieved. Some say success is gained by luck; some say it is earned by diligence and effort; others say it is achieved by continued accumulation and persistence...Obviously we cannot deny all these definitions, but at the same time we have to accept that "success= a good team + a sound mechanism + diligence and effort + continued persistence".

CNOOD's partnership system that is "created, shared and managed by all" has become the top-level planning for her success in business. And the enthusiasm and passion in every CNOODer, their perseverance and the perfection-seeking character, and the corporate philosophy of "Pristine Simplicity, Amorphous Unity, Reciprocal Constancy", have been added together to build the great CNOOD family.

There were quarrels and conflicts between project members from both parties during our project. But instead of shirking responsibilities, we always worked together to find solutions. This is because we share a common goal, that is, to do a good job in every project, maintain high quality of products, make every product made in China a top-notch one and achieve the first rate in the world. This is why we insist a quality requirement

stricter than the average standard for products in the industry. Conformity to standards is only our bottom line; what we are aiming is to achieve excellency.

比如，最近成功完成的克罗地亚佩列沙茨大桥项目，施璐德作为大桥管桩解决方案提供方，为 EPC 总承包方在欧洲承接的第一座跨海大桥奠定坚实的基础，而莱茵与施璐德同心协力，克服业主设计修改多，施工难度大，按 EN1090 EXC4 欧洲最高焊接标准要求，以及北方冬季环境恶劣等不利因素，保证了三批都高质量、如期发运，受到 EPC 和业主的好评，成为"一带一路"倡议和"16+1 合作"等框架下的典范。

Take the recently completed Peljesac Bridge in Croatia. As the supplier of piles solution, CNOON laid a solid foundation for the EPC general contractor's first cross-sea bridge in Europe. TÜV Rheinland and CNOOD worked together and overcame the difficulties brought about by unfavorable conditions, including the many amendments made by the owner, highly difficult construction, conformity requirement of EN1090 EXC4 welding standard, and the harsh winter in the northern area. We assured the high-quality, timely shipment of three batches of products, and was well received by the

EPC contractor and the owner, becoming a model within the framework of "Belt and Road" Initiative and the "16+1 Cooperation".

I get to know a lot of people at CNOOD, who always greet me with big smiles at the CNOOD office. Every one of them is full of positive energy and enjoys working. Here at CNOOD, some get love, some achieve success in study, some gain

在施璐德，结识了很多人，每次去施璐德办公室，他们脸上都充满笑容跟你打招呼，看到他们每个人身上都充满了正能量。他们每个人都在享受着工作，在这里他们有人收获了爱情，有人收获了学业，有人收获了事业，有人收获了大满贯，每个人都有着自己的精彩故事。

　　工作和生活有时确实会让我们感到很累，但这个世界不会因为你的疲惫，而停下它的脚步。如果真的觉得累，不要停下来，想想自己的梦想和自己的初衷，继续走下去，未来一定是充满了喜悦和成功，相互成就，彼此装饰我们的梦！

success in career, and yet some win the "Grand Slam." Everyone has an exciting story of his/her own.

Sometimes we indeed become tired because of the burdens of work and life; however, the world would not stop its footsteps because you are tired. If you really feel tired, don't stop. Think about your dream and original aspirations and move on. Future is bound to be filled with joy and success. Let's be mutually fulfilling and adorn the dreams of each other.

王 豪
David Wang

金属材料专业本科，MBA 工商管理硕士。第三方检测认证行业从业 11 年，曾就职于三家不同国际检测认证公司。现任德国莱茵 TUV 工业服务工业检验部门经理。

David graduated from college majoring in Metal Material Engineering and holds an MBA degree. He has 11 years of working experience in third party inspection (TPI) and worked for three international inspection firms. He is currently a manager at the Industrial Inspection Department, Industrial Service Stream, TÜV Rheinland.

心若不死，便有未来
Future Is There So Long As the Heart Lives On

■ Michael Wang

2014年12月，在油气价格急剧跌落的那个冬天，我有幸作为国民油井华南通基地的质量经理为Dennis、Fay、Tiger和其他几名施璐德合伙人介绍了国民油井华高陆地钻机的生产制造流程，当天介绍结束便与我的搭档做完交接工作离开现

In December 2014, the winter season during which oil prices had a sharp decline, I was lucky to have the opportunity, as a quality manager from the Nantong Base of National Oilwell Varco (NOV), to give a presentation about

场。正是那天的契缘与巧合，萌生了后来我加入施璐德的情怀。2018 年 6 月的夏天，我离开了曾经一直引以为傲的公司，正式加入施璐德的大家庭，成为 QEHS 部门的一员。

曾几何时，对自己的职业规划自信满满，想要毕生致力于油气能源行业。没想到的是，经历过 2012 为期 2 年油价最后的疯狂后，从 2014 年末到 2018 年初油价的跌宕起伏，曾经我那豪情壮志的誓言已经渐渐地湮灭在我内心的深处。猛然间，我前方的路，开始变得茫然……

the manufacturing process of NOV land rigs for Dennis, Fay, Tiger and other CNOOD partners. After the presentation I handed the job over to my colleague and left the project site. It is the chance created by that occasion that gave birth to my wish to join CNOOD. In June 2018, I left the company which I had always been proud of and joined the CNOOD family as a member of its QEHS department.

I used to be extremely confident about my career plan and made up my mind to devote myself to the oil and gas industry for the rest of my life. However, the period between the end of 2014 and the beginning of 2018 saw unexpected fluctuations in oil prices after the two-year final frenzy around the year 2012. My lofty sentiments and high aspirations gradually disappeared at the bottom of my heart. All of a sudden, the road ahead of me became vague...

加入施璐德大家庭近1年的时间里，深感于施璐德的人文情怀。记得加入施璐德的第一个星期，在陪同 Fay 拜访客户的展示过程中，聆听了 Fay 对施璐德文化介绍的时候，感动得热泪盈眶，内心的澎湃久久不能平静，暗自轻声问一句，"这样的公司不就是我想要的吗"？在后续的介绍当中，更多的了解到施璐德的发展业务范围后，猛然间，我又重新看到了曙光，感受到了那久违的温暖……

加入施璐德近一年的时光里，生活过得紧张而又充实，有感于身边的同事敬业、好学、肯干、团结协作的精神，自己自然也不得有任何放松与懈怠，重新点燃了我大学刚毕业那会"初生牛犊不怕虎"的斗志与激情，与这群志同道合的小伙伴们一起追逐内心的梦。

I have been deeply touched by its people-oriented culture since I joined CNOOD nearly one year ago. I still remember the time when I listened to Fay's introduction of CNOOD's corporate culture during a visit to our client during the first week after I joined CNOOD and was moved to tears, asking myself with great excitement, "Isn't it THE company that I have been looking for?" In her following presentation, I learned more about the business lines of CNOOD. All of a sudden, I saw the daylight again and felt a warmth that I hadn't experienced for a long time.

My life has been busy and full since I joined CNOOD. Moved by my colleagues' devotion to work, their eagerness to learn, and their diligence and the spirit of cooperation, I have never allowed myself to slack even in the slightest degree. In pursuing the heart dream together with my colleagues who share common ambitions and aspirations, I kindle again the youthful fearlessness and the fighting spirit I once had when I graduated from

是的，我们每个人内心都有各自的梦，但作为施璐德人我们都有一个共同的梦，那个梦想值得我们每一个施璐德人为之倾心、为之努力。感谢 Dennis 和 Fay 在这个梦想的舞台上为我们点亮了前行的路，感谢施璐德的每一位小伙伴们的信任、包容、理解和关爱，让我能够在为之热爱的事业领域里纵横驰骋，为之倾心、为之付出！

"长风破浪会有时，直挂云帆济沧海"！奋斗前行的路上，感恩有你！

college.

Yes, every one of us has a unique dream, but we as CNOODers share a common dream, a dream which we fall in love with and work hard for. Our gratitude goes to Dennis and Fay who illuminate the road ahead for us. I would also thank every member at CNOOD for their trust, forgiveness, understanding and caring love, which enables me to fully realize my potential and devote myself to a cause which I love so much.

"A time will come to ride the wind and cleave the waves; I'll set my cloud-white sail and cross the sea which raves." I am grateful to having you with me when marching forward.

王 坤
Michael Wang

王坤，1986 年 7 月出生于福建南平，2009 年毕业于南昌航空大学，测控技术与仪器专业，学士学位。ISO 内审员、国家质量技术监督局特种设备注册检验师，美国无损检测学会高级检验师、美国腐蚀工程协会检验师、美国焊接协会检验师，IPMP 国际项目经理资质，上海市注册安全生产管理人员。毕业以后一直任职于制造领域的相关外企，主要负责质量和技术工作。

Michael was born in Nanping, Fujian Province in July 1986. He graduated from Nanchang Hangkong University (NCHU) with a B.Sc. in Measurement & Control Technology and Instrumentation. He is an ISO quality management systems internal auditor, and a special equipment inspector registered in State Bureau of Quality and Technology Supervision. He is also a senior inspector certified by American Society for Nondestructive Testing (ASNT), an inspector certified by National Association of Corrosion Engineers (NACE), and a welding inspector certified by American Welding Society (AWS). He is International Project Manager Professional (IPMP) and a registered work safety manager in Shanghai. He worked for foreign-owned manufacturing enterprises after graduation and has focused on quality-and technology-related jobs.

博观·约取·创作
See More, Take Less, and Write Creatively

■ Tony Liu

博观者，开拓视野，增广见闻，普阅周天之事，遍识周天之物。心无狭隘，思无障碍。譬若读书，读经不恶世俗，读子明辨万象，读史自省知理，读诗见性明心。至于行路，行路读书，知行合一，本来一物；博学于文，笃行于道。

约取者，取其精华，去其糟粕，有所为有所不为。非博观无以约取，非约取无以博观。必先知而后爱，博观是启蒙之基；生有涯学无涯，约取乃博观之要。

To see more is to broaden your vision, enrich your experience, have a look at everything in the universe and possess a thorough knowledge of them. You will then be able to get rid of narrow-mindedness, and become a free thinker. Take reading for example: Reading Confucian classics gives you worldly wisdom; philosophical works, fine discernment; history, the ability to conduct self-examination and find the Truth; poems, an introspective perception of your nature. As for travelling, it is, with the unity of knowledge and practice, naturally much the same as reading. Being widely versed in culture, you should practice the Way with all your heart.

To take less is to absorb the essence and discard the dross. There are things you should do and things you shouldn't. You are unable to take less until you see

创作者，究天人之际，通古今之变，成一家之言。

more, and unable to see more unless you take less. One must first acquire knowledge before he can love, so it is the foundation of enlightenment to see more. Zhuangzi, the famous Chinese philosopher lived during the Warring States period, says, "There is a limit to our lives, but to knowledge there is no limit." Therefore, it is of fundamental importance to take less when you try to see more.

To write creatively is to investigate the laws of Nature and human affairs, understand thoroughly the changes of ancient and modern times, and become a school of thought of your own.

修学储能,厚积薄发。无论爱什么——饭、异性、国、民族、人类等等,只有纠缠如毒蛇,执著如怨鬼,二六时中,没有已时者有望(引自鲁迅《华盖集·杂感》)。

Be fully prepared in both knowledge and ability, and you will achieve success. "Whatever you love—food, the opposite sex, your country, the nation, mankind—you can only hope to win it if you cling to it like a poisonous snake, seize hold of it like an avenging spirit, and never slacken your efforts for one moment." (Lu Xun, "Stray Thoughts", *Bad Luck*.)

刘 彬
Tony Liu

刘彬,别名观棋柯烂,好古文,寄情于松桂云壑。毕业于上海大学,2016年加入施璐德。

Tony, aka "A Woodcutter Watching the Chess Game Long Ago", is fond of Chinese ancient proses and finds enjoyment in natural scenery such as "pine trees, sweet-scented osmanthus, and valleys shrouded in clouds". He graduated from Shanghai University and joined CNOOD in 2016.

岁月与梦想

Times and Dream

■ Echo Lee

岁月

时间就像一条河流，
载着我们顺流而下，
遇到现实，需要决策，
但我们无法停留，
也无法回避，
只能以最好的方式应对。

——Ray Dalio

很早以前，我就开始思考，我所做的事情，我所去到的地方，我所遇到的人，究竟哪些才对我的生命具有真正重要的意义；后来我才逐渐明白，原来所有的一切并不是它们本身有意义，而是你觉得它有意义，就像《小王子》中那独一无二的玫瑰花。

Times

Time is like a river
that will take you forward
into encounters with reality that will require you to make decisions.
You can't stop the movement down this river,
and you can't avoid the encounters.
You can only approach these encounters in the best way possible.
—Ray Dalio

I began to think, long ago, which of the things I did, the places I visited and the persons I met would have truly important meaning for my life. It is in later days that I am beginning to understand that one thing becomes important not because it is meaningful by itself, but because you consider it to be meaningful, just as in the case of the

2018年，是我在施璐德度过的第六年。回顾过去，在我记忆中闪闪发亮的，是那些竭尽全力奋斗的时光，那些承载了我梦想的地方，和那些陪我一起奋斗的人们。

"盛开的向日葵"

2013年3月，我在施璐德实习两月有余，开始了人生中的第一次跟单。在中午十二点的海润仓库，同事说我像个向日葵。

unique rose in *The Little Prince.*

2018 is the sixth year that I have spent at CNOOD. Looking back on the past, what glisten in my memory are the times when I worked as hard as I could, the place which carried my dreams, and people who endeavored side by side with me.

"A Sunflower in Full Bloom"

It was my first time to follow an order in March 2013, after I had been working at CNOOD as an intern for more than two months. It was 12:00 at the Hairun Warehouse, they said that I was like a sunflower.

"我想当海盗"

2014 年 11 月,天津港。

我站在岸边看着吊机下的夕阳,突然觉得这画面充满了工业的力量。

在不允许女生上船的奇葩规定下,我想,能每天欣赏这样的风景,海盗也是很幸福的!

"灯塔"

2015 年新年第一天,夜晚的静安寺就像我心中的灯塔。

"I wanna be a pirate"

It was in November 2014, at Tianjin Port.

Standing on the shore and looking at the sun setting under the cranes, I suddenly felt that it was an image full of industrial force.

It is a weird rule that women are not allowed to go aboard a cargo ship. It would be happy even to be a pirate, I thought, if I could enjoy such scenery every day!

"A lighthouse"

On the first day of the coming 2015, Jing'an Temple, against the darkness of the sky, was like a lighthouse in my eyes.

"一场不能输的战斗"

2016年8月，四十几度的车间挥汗如雨。忍不能忍，为的是团队的目标，成就的却是自己的内心。目送最后一车远走，夜幕下的尘土飞扬是最美的风景。

"我的宝贝"

2017年11月，我的宝贝女儿悠悠来到了这个世界。紧握的小拳头似乎在对我说："妈妈，加油！"

"A battle that we cannot lose"

In August 2016, I dripped with sweat in the workshop with a temperature of above 40 degree Celsius. It was for the team's goal that I tried to tolerate something that was hard to bear. Meanwhile, I fulfilled my inner calling. Seeing off the last truck, the flying dust in the darkness of night was the most beautiful scene to me.

"My baby girl"

In November 2017, my baby girl Yoyo came to this world. Clenching her little fist, she seemed to say to me, "Come on, Mom!"

"职场妈妈元年"

2018年3月，我正式成为一名职场新妈妈。女儿激励我前行！

"The First Year as a Working Mom"

In March 2018, I became a fresh working mom. I was inspired by my daughter to ever move ahead!

梦想

进化是宇宙中最强大的力量，
是唯一永恒的东西，
是生命最大的成就，
和最大的回报。

——Ray Dalio

Dream

I believe that evolution... is the greatest single force in the universe.

I believe that the desire to evolve, i.e., to get better, is probably humanity's most pervasive driving force.

Personally, I believe that personal evolution is both the greatest accomplishment and the greatest reward.

——Ray Dalio

在施璐德的这六年，无疑是我人生中最黄金的六年。因为这是在对世界，对自己，都具备了相对成熟的认知后做出的选

The six years at CNOOD has so far doubtlessly been the most golden years in my life. It was a choice I made after I had

择；也是从学生向成熟职场人转变的关键时期。

这六年中所遇到的每一个人，经历的每一件事，参与的每一个项目，点点滴滴积累成如今对于行业，对于社会，对于自己的目标和梦想的思考与认识；施璐德的文化和风格，也早已内化成了我为人处世的原则。

2018年，生活带来的角色转变让我产生了更多的思考，努力跳出固有的视角，从更宏观的层面来审视自己，总结过去并为自己人生的新篇章做规划。

以前我以为这六年最重要的收获是行业经验的积累，但随着视角的改变，我开始发现，成长型的思维，才是我在施璐德

a relatively mature understanding of the world as well as of myself. Moreover, it was a critical period when I transformed myself from a college student to a senior at workplace.

Every person I met, every occasion I experienced, and every project I took part in during the six years have all been added up together, bit by bit, to form my understanding of the industry, the society, and my goals and dream. The corporate culture and style of CNOOD has long become an intrinsic part of me.

In 2018, the shift of roles in my life made me think more, get rid of stereotyped perspective, review myself from a broader horizon, make a summary of the past days, and chart a blueprint for my future growth.

I used to think that the industrial experiences accumulated was the most important asset for me during the six

成长的六年中，得到的最宝贵的财富。

在施璐德的前三年，我就像一部高速运转的机器，忙得没有停下来思考的时间；我感觉非常良好，每一天都在迎接新的挑战，战胜新的困难；我不执著于努力的结果，因为每一件事情都让我感觉新奇，哪怕掉到坑里，我都享受坠落的感觉。

进入第四年，心态在不知不觉间发生了微妙的变化，那是一种基于自我定位提升带来的期望值的转变。我不再那么享受失败，没有获得结果的努力让我感到痛苦；竭尽全力冲刺后的失败，就像赛场上输给一个旗鼓相当的对手，一盘棋有时候可以铭记十年。也就是在这个时候，施璐德的文化对我潜意识的影响开始逐步显现，只是我还不自知。

又经历了两年的磨炼，如今站在第七年的起点，我已经足够自信能够超越上一阶段的自己，同时也更清醒地认识到帮助自己成功跨越的这种力量。

"跟随内心，做最好的自己。"不只是一种口号，而是一种人生态度。施璐德公司本身，就是这一理念的践行者。从产品

years. With the changing of viewpoint, however, I have begun to notice that a growth-oriented way of thinking is the most valuable treasure I have got during my six years of growth at CNOOD.

During the first three years, I was like a fast-operating machine, too busy to have a stop for thinking. At that time I was feeling good, and was embracing new challenges and overcoming difficulties every day. I was not obsessed with the result of effort, because everything was new in my eyes. I would even enjoy the falling if I dropped into a pit.

In the fourth year, my state of mind had a subtle change even before I noticed it. That was a change of expectation based on the enhanced self-positioning. I no longer enjoy the feeling of failure so much, and would be greatly agonized by fruitless effort. Being defeated after an exhausting spurt is just like being defeated by an equal opponent in a *go* game, which could in some cases be remembered for ten years. It was then that the influence of the CNOOD culture on my subconsciousness began to show itself, while I was unaware of it.

After two more years of testing, I am now at the threshold of the seventh year. I am confident enough to surpass my old self, and at the same time have a clearer understanding of the force that has helped me succeed in achieving this.

"Follow the heart, and be your best self" is more than a slogan; it's an attitude toward life. CNOOD is a company that

升级到模式转变，不守成，不停歇，不胆怯，不设限；强大的内在进化驱动力是公司不断跨越台阶的核心竞争力。也是在这股浪潮的席卷下，进化的动力打破了我固有的胜负观，终于能够站在更宽广的角度来理解这个世界，理解自己在世界中的位置，也对自己的未来有了不同的期待。

我更有信心面对生活中的各种约束条件，我开始相信"妈妈"这个新角色未必是我职场生涯的减分项，也不会是我梦想的拦路石。

而我的梦想，也不再是一个具体的目标。我想要去掉潜意识中给自己的设限，去做一个更好更强大的自己。机遇和运气就像天气，而我将风雨无阻。

put this idea into action. From product upgrading to the shift of business model, it does not stick to the old way, does not stop and look, does not become timid, nor set any limitations. The powerful innate driving force is CNOOD's core competitiveness in continuously being ever stronger. Pushed forward by this trend, the evolutionary force has put an end to my old viewpoint of what is success and what is failure. It has enabled me to finally understand the world and my position in it from a broader perspective, while having a different expectation for my future development.

I am more confident in facing the various restrictions in life. I am beginning to believe that the new role of "mom" is not necessarily something negative to my career, nor will it be a stumbling block in fulfilling my dream.

And my dream is no longer limited to a specific objective. I want to remove the restrictions in my subconsciousness and become a better, stronger person. Chances and luck are like the weather, and I am determined to go forward through storms.

李天竹
Echo Lee

复旦大学经济学硕士，2013年毕业后正式加入施璐德，开启了激情澎湃的岁月。爱好哲学，喜欢思考人生。
升级成为妈妈后，享受工作和家庭间角色转换的乐趣。
Echo Lee received her M. Econ. from Fudan University and joined CNOOD after graduation. At CNOOD she started a period of passionate, exciting years. She is fond of philosophy and likes thinking about life. After becoming a mom, infant care now becomes the thing she loves most. She enjoys her shifting roles at work and home.

眼观日月，心入江河

See the Sun and Moon with Your Eyes, and Let Your Heart Merge into the Rivers

■ Echo Lee

几乎每一个人都思考过人生的意义。

可能是在懵懂的孩童时期，可能是在考场失利的困顿时期，可能是长辈的一场葬礼，也可能是太阳初升于海平面的那一刹那。

我们的思绪在那一瞬间停留，感受着那一刻的存在，并思考它的意义。但是很快，匆忙的脚步掩盖了瞬间的思绪，那一刻寂然的存在湮没在碌碌日常琐碎之中。

但是，总有一抹朦胧的光，让我们的灵魂朝向那个方向。

那里有一个遥不可及的终点：

释迦摩尼在一棵菩提树下最终到达了

Almost every one of us has pondered over the meaning of life:

Maybe in your childhood when you barely knew anything; maybe at the hard time when you failed in an exam; maybe during a funeral of one of your elders; or maybe at the moment when the sun rises above the horizon.

We stopped thinking at that very moment, beginning to feel the existence of that moment and consider its meaning. But our transient train of thought was soon concealed by hasty steps, with the silent existence of that moment buried among the daily trivialities.

However, there is always a vague hint of light, toward which our souls are attracted.

There is a destination too far for us to reach:

Sakyamuni eventually reached there

那里；

庄生在变为蝴蝶的遨游中融入了那个所在；

孔子用"仁"来描述这种境界；

耶稣用自己的受难来完成这份救赎。

智慧如斯，对于人生终极问题的描述却如此迥然不同。

真相是什么？

实际上，每一位参透人生真谛的智者，都是在其所处的时空中，在当下的情景中，尽量用当时人们能够理解的语言来阐述他的领悟，并上升为指导人们思想和生活的理论或教义。

然而，思想的迷雾是如此的变化多端，以至于古往今来集人类智慧大成的智者们耗尽毕生心血，也难以将其智慧为芸芸众生所领悟。

终极的智慧是如此的不可描述，以至于超出了语言的界限。因此，古代先贤就似在对一个盲人描述一头大象一样，有的从鼻子开始说起，有的从耳朵开始说起；虽然最终描述的都是大象，但在整体描述的过程中，采用了不同的叙事方法和逻辑。又因为真相的不可描述性，隐喻与象征的手法频繁使用。

beneath a bodhi tree;

Zhuangzi merged himself into that state of being in the dream of becoming a butterfly;

Confucius used "Benevolence" to describe that state;

Jesus Christ accomplished this redemption by his crucifixion.

Wise men as they were, their answers to the ultimate questions of life were utterly different.

What is then truth?

In fact, every wise man who gains a thorough understanding of the true meaning of life has tried, within the specific time and space, to explain his understanding by a language easy enough for his contemporaries, and lift it up to be a theory or doctrine which provides guidance for people's thought and life.

However, the mist of human thoughts is so varied that the great wise men throughout the history spent all their lives and yet cannot make their wisdom be understood by all mortal beings.

The ultimate wisdom is indescribable to such an extent that it goes beyond the limit of language. The sages of ancient times, therefore, were just like the six blind men who described the elephant: One started from its nose, and another from its ears. Though they were talking about the same elephant, they used different ways of narration and logic in describing it as a whole. And due to the indescribability of truth, metaphor and symbolism were frequently used.

听的人就易据此形成各自的流派，并对于描述细节深入解读，讨论和争辩；一旦把隐喻和象征作为金科玉律，思想就失去了生命力，成为了教条。

社会的发展是如此的一日千里，以至于每个时代产生的问题无法再套用教条的理论来理解。

因此对于伟大先贤智慧的理解，正确的方法莫过于王阳明所说的"因时致治"。将开悟之道融入现代世界的车水马龙之中，此谓之传承。

站在现代科技基石之上，当代人类的生活状态是前人难以想象的。

人类对于外在世界的探究，处于史无前例的高度。

航天学的发展使得人类能够探索星辰之外的遥远天际；

量子力学的发展引导了一系列重大高新科技变革；

基因科学的发展一再攻克疑难疾病；

人工智能计算机已在多个领域战胜复杂的人脑。

科技进步的好处，显而易见。

Listeners were then prone to be divided into different groups according to the different ways, and made in-depth inquiry, discussion and debate regarding the details. Once the metaphor and symbolism were taken as the golden rule, human thinking loses its vitality and becomes mere dogma.

The society moves on at so quick a pace that we could not expect to understand the problems of any age by mechanically applying dogmatic theories.

As a result, the correct way of understanding the wisdom of the great sages is, as Wang Yangming put it, "to achieve order in the light of the trend of times." It is called "heritage" when we integrate the Way of enlightenment into the bustling modern world.

Based on modern science and technology, the present-day human life is hard to imagine for our ancestors.

Human beings are now at an unprecedented height in their exploration of the outside world.

The development of astronautics enables men to explore the remotest part of the universe beyond the stars;

The development of quantum mechanics leads to a series of major high-tech breakthroughs;

The development of genetic science helps to cure complicated diseases again and again;

AI computers have defeated the complex human brains in various fields.

The merits of technological progress

当我们舒适的坐在人类历史上最快速的交通工具上,用手机安排远在千里之外的各种事务时,我们对于世界有着前所未有的掌控感。但正是这种看似强大的力量,使我们对外界的依赖上升到了史无前例的高度,反求内心的必要性在人类科技的狂欢中变得无足轻重。

直到生活中某个不和谐的音符打断高速行驶的理性列车。

那份戛然而止的静默感让我们猝不及防。

内心的虚弱和无力也以前所未有的能量吞噬着我们的灵魂。

但问题并不在于科学本身,而是如此快速的进步,使得生存与社会之中的人,未能及时在心灵层面得到同等速度的滋养,得以匹配并享用这份现代科技的盛宴。

一百多年前,尼采在《瓦格纳事件》中说:"在自己的身上克服他的时代,成为无时代的人。这是对哲学家的最低要求,也是最高要求。"

这一精辟的论断,不但是对哲学家的要求,也是我们这个时代获得内心平静和

are obvious to all of us.

When we sit comfortably in the fastest vehicles ever in human history and arrange business thousands of miles away, we are having an unprecedented sense of control over the world. However, it is this seemingly powerful strength that has made us more dependent on the outside than ever. The necessity to turn back and seek our heart becomes insignificant among the carnival of human technology.

Things go on like that until the high-speed train of Reason is interrupted by some nasty note in our life.

We are then taken by surprise because of the sudden silence.

In the meantime, the frailty and weakness within us are devouring our souls with an unprecedented energy.

But we should not blame science itself. The problem is: With such rapid progress, people living in the society are not nourished at an equivalent speed in their mind and soul to be able to enjoy this feast of modern science and technology.

More than one hundred years ago, Friedrich Nietzsche wrote in "The Case of Wagner" (Der Fall Wagner):

Was verlangt ein Philosoph am ersten und letzten von sich? Seine Zeit in sich zu überwinden, „zeitlos" zu werden. (What does a philosopher demand of himself first and last? To overcome his time in himself, to become "timeless.")

His excellent remark is not only a requirement for philosophers but also an

领悟人生真谛的良方。

克服这个时代，也就是通过内省外察来冲破其加之于自身的局限性，那个从时代中抽离出来的自我，才代表了真理的方向。

科学是一门以物质世界为基础的学科，这一性质决定了其研究方法必然是着眼于外在客观世界，而非内在精神世界。在科学凯歌高奏的百余年来，其对现实世界的巨大影响已经使得科学成为了一种信仰，以至于内在精神世界受到前所未有的

effective remedy for acquiring inner peace and understanding the true meaning of life in our era.

"To overcome the time" means to break, through introspection and observation the limitations imposed by it upon us. It is THAT self which has been isolated from the time that represents the direction toward truth.

The fact that science is based on the material world has determined the focus of its research methodology on the outside objective world rather than the inside mental world. In the past hundred years which witnessed its great triumph,

忽视。

但如果把历史镜头再拉长到千年，就会发现一个现代人难以想象的场景：人类对于内心世界的信仰和探索，曾经占据着压倒性的优势。

人类智慧是一个多维的存在。外在世界和内心体验，是一枚硬币的两个面，在无休止的旋转中交汇，融合，形成不息的生命之河，奔腾的河水是迅猛前进的科学技术，延绵起伏的地势是心灵力量的承托。

科学的目的并非让我们远离内心，而是在百转千回后蓦然回首；生命的答案不在遥远的银河深处，而是存在于每个人的心中。

尽管我们从小所受的教育集中在认识外在世界，却很少涉及内心体验；

尽管内在世界难以交流，内在经验难以验证；

尽管每个人的内心都是一座孤岛。

但是，我们的内心在造物主神秘力量

science has become a faith because of its huge influence on the real world. As a result, our inner mental world is neglected to an unprecedented extent.

If we extend the historical perspective further back to one thousand years ago, however, we will see something hard to imagine for people living in modern times: Men's conviction and inquiry of their inner world once enjoyed an overwhelming advantage.

Human wisdom is a multi-dimensional being. The outside world and your inner experience are the two sides of a coin, intermingling and merging into each other in incessant whirls. The ceaseless River of Life is then formed: The rushing stream is the fast developing science and technology, while the rolling surface of earth is the supporting power of the soul.

The purpose of science is not to make us go further away from our heart, but turn back after thousands of twists; the answer of life does not lie in the depth of the Galaxy, but in the heart of everyone.

Though we were educated since childhood to focus on knowing the world outside us instead of our inner experience;

Though it is hard to carry out communication between inner worlds and to verify inner experience;

Though the heart of anyone is an island entirely of itself: —

We have a need to find ourselves

的驱使下,有着向内找回自己的需要。

因此,终归有一天,在享受了科技的暴雨之后,我们还会回到心灵的原点。

所以我们会在某些瞬间想到生死,想到人生的意义。

所以那些相隔数千年的声音,至今依然撞击着我们的心灵。

古有先贤曰:修身,齐家,治国,平天下。

不是境界差异,唯同一颗心而已。

again, inspired by the mysterious power of the Creator.

Therefore, one day we shall go back to the spiritual origin after enjoying the storms of science and technology.

So at certain moments we will think of the question of life and death, and the meaning of living.

And the voices thousands of years ago are still striking our souls today.

The old teaching says, "A true gentleman should cultivate his person, regulate his family, rightly govern his state, and then the world will be given peace."

It is not the difference of levels. After all, we share the same heart.

这颗心修炼到通透,独处便是修身,为人子女父母便是齐家,为国家计则是治国,为众生传道即是平天下。

能够时时觉察内心,静观意念和情绪起落,抽离并超脱,按天理行事,是为修身;

能够在与家人相处时,时刻反观内心,不被别人所思所想遮云蔽目,是为齐家;

能够克除私欲,将己身置于时代洪流中审时度势,顺势而为,是为治国;

能够将真理融入时代,将一己之心扩大为天下心,是为平天下。

回顾一下自己的人生经历,那些曾经让人刻骨铭心的事件,如何成就了如今的我们。

那些曾经为之欣喜若狂的成果早已不再影响我们的生活,但为之奋斗的岁月仍在记忆中闪闪发光;

那些曾经为之思虑、纠结、计较和担忧的事件,早已如浮云一般离我们远去,

When the heart is trained to the supremacy, one can "cultivate his person" by being alone, "regulate his family" by being a member of it, "rightly govern his state" by acting to the interests of the country, and "give peace to the world" by spreading the teachings for people.

He who is able to be aware of his heart at any time, calmly observe the fluctuation of ideas and emotions while getting rid of them, and act according to the heavenly principles is regarded as "cultivating his person."

He who is able to take an introspective view of himself when being with his family and is never blinded by the thoughts of others is regarded as "regulating his family."

He who is able to remove selfish desires, put himself in the great tide of times and act according to the trends is regarded as "rightly governing his state."

He who is able to integrate truth into his times and extend the heart of the self to the heart of the world is regarded as "giving peace to the world."

Look back on your life experience and think again how those unforgettable events have shaped what we are today.

The achievements for which we were once wild with joy have long ceased to impact our lives. Nevertheless the days during which we worked hard for these achievements are still glistening in our memories.

The events about which we used to be concerned, hesitant, fussy or anxious

但那份感受却祭奠成我们人生的道路。

人事思虑两岸过，唯有吾心入江河。

生活是最温柔，也是最严厉的老师。未能完成的功课，一定反复出现；无论你有多么想要逃避，都无处可藏；如果不能够真正超越，它就一直存留在那里。直到你从心底容纳了它，吸收了它，它才会转化为前进的动力，让心灵向另一个层面成长。

所以，让我们以坦然的心态面对生活中的一切好的，坏的，用智慧去转化它，而不是让它加重自己的人生底色。渐渐的我们的心就会变得更加柔软和通透，走出狭窄的空间，踏入生命的河流。

无论哪个时代，人生不过就是完成一些艰难的功课，途中遇到一些值得纪念的人，最终迎来属于我们的极致风景。

罗素在《如何平静老去》中，如此描述这一风景：

"每一个人的生活都应该像河水一样——开始是细小的，被限制在狭窄的两岸之间，然后热烈地冲过巨石，滑下瀑布。渐渐地，河道变宽了，河岸扩展了，河水流得更平稳了。最后，河水流入了海洋，不再有明显的间断和停顿，而后便毫

have gone away from us like the floating clouds. However, these feelings have helped to build the roads in our life.

"With the worldly concerns and anxieties I go through the two banks; my heart alone merges into the river."

Life is the gentlest and yet sternest teacher. The schoolwork you have not finished will come up repeatedly. You have no place to hide yourself however hard you try to. It will remain there if you fail to surpass it in the real sense of the word. It will be transformed into a driving force for moving ahead and enable your soul to grow toward another level only when you have accepted and assimilated it from the bottom of your heart.

Therefore, let's face whatever is good or bad in our life with a calm mind, and, instead of allowing it to darken our lives, transform it by wisdom. Gradually our heart will become gentler and more enlightened, enabling us to go out of the narrow space and into the River of Life.

Whatever era we are in, life is but to finish some difficult schoolwork, to meet some people who are worthy to be remembered, and finally to see our own ultimate sceneries.

Bertrand Russell described the scene in his essay "How to Grow Old":

An individual human existence should be like a river - small at first, narrowly contained within its banks, and rushing passionately past rocks and over waterfalls. Gradually the river grows wider, the banks recede, the waters flow more quietly, and in the end, without any

无痛苦地摆脱了自身的存在。"

在儒家文化体系中，这一风景被更加言简意赅的描述为："天人合一。"

visible break, they become merged in the sea, and painlessly lose their individual being.

This scene, in the Confucianist doctrine, is summarized in a more succinct way as "the unification of the Heaven and mankind."

李天竹
Echo Lee

复旦大学经济学硕士，2013年毕业后正式加入施璐德，开启了激情澎湃的岁月。爱好哲学，喜欢思考人生。升级成为妈妈后，享受工作和家庭间角色转换的乐趣。

Echo Lee received her M. Econ. from Fudan University and joined CNOOD after graduation. At CNOOD she started a period of passionate, exciting years. She is fond of philosophy and likes thinking about life. After becoming a mom, infant care now becomes the thing she loves most. She enjoys her shifting roles at work and home.

人生的智慧

The Wisdom of Life

■ Johnson Shen

闲暇时间，总会考虑该做点什么，除了那些不可避免的应酬外，也许一本书一杯茶更适合我度过消遣时光。

也正因为如此，时常会看到当今社会对于人类阅读的呼吁，经常拿中国人和外国人的阅读量作对比，以此来说明中国的下一代正步入知识的贫穷。

总体来说，2018 年我的阅读量也是远远不够的，期间给自己找了许许多多的借口，或是出差，或是家庭，或是聚会。总而言之，每每会以一种让自己心满意足的理由去逃避阅读，即便是偶有坐在书桌前，也是味同嚼蜡，犹如行尸走肉一般。这种感觉让我很难受，内心的矛盾总让我不知所措，后悔的感觉也时常萦绕心头。

At my leisure I would always consider what I should do. It seems to me that, except for necessary social engagements, a book and a cup of tea are the most suitable for me to spend my free time.

From time to time, therefore, I notice a public appeal to people to read more books. Citizens' average amount of reading in China is often compared with that in Western countries to show that our next generation is beginning to experience the knowledge poverty.

On the whole, my amount of reading in 2018 was far from enough. I would find various excuses for myself: business trips, family affairs, or parties. In a word, I always try to evade reading with a reason that satisfied me. Even when I occasionally sat down before the desk, I was completely spiritless and found the books insipid. This made me feel uncomfortable. I was always totally

bewildered by my conflicting thoughts and the feeling of regret hovered in my mind.

然而在很久很久以前,阅读从来就不是一件大事,甚至很多人都提出不要盲目的阅读,要更多的思考。之前阅读过叔本华的著作《人生的智慧》,初看题目,我本以为它是单纯地讲述思考的重要性和意义的,才读了几句便发现他的重点似乎并不在此。作者从某种程度上来说批判了毫无目的和思考的阅读,也就是说看似否定了我们这个时代的一些观点。

A long time ago, however, reading was not a big thing at all. Quite a few people even reminded us that we should not read blindly and should spend more time on thinking. Previously I read Arthur Schopenhauer's *The Wisdom of Life*, whose title, at first glance, made me believe it's a book purely concerns the importance and implications of thinking. I realized this is not its real point shortly after I finished the first several sentences in it. The author, to a certain extent, criticized aimless reading without thinking, and thus seemed to have refuted some of the ideas in the modern era.

阅读终究只是外来物,毕竟已只是思考的基础,而真正独立思考的人才是在精神上的君主。哪怕是再大的图书馆,如果

Reading is after all something outside us; it lays the foundation for thinking, and yet no more than that. Only

它藏书丰富但却杂乱无章，其实际用处反不如那些规模虽小却条理井然的图书馆。同样，如果一个人拥有大量的知识，却未经过自己头脑的独立思考而加以吸收，那么这些学识就远不如那些虽所知不多但却经过认真思考的知识有价值。

阅读可以随意，而思考却不能随意，只有当一个人把他的所知结合各方面来考察，把每一真知相互比照之后，他才能真正理解、掌握这些知识，并使其为己所用。因为一个人只能对自己知道的事情加以仔细思考，所以他必须要学习新东西；但是，也只有那些经过深思熟虑的东西才能成为他的真知。

或许这些道理大家都明白，但为何此时此刻，社会却鲜有谈论？

似乎我们这个时代只顾着呼吁阅读的数量，却忘了阅读的质量。

其实并非如此，时代发生着改变，在叔本华的时代，人们并没有过多的娱乐条件，而不想动脑子的打发时间之事似乎只剩下了阅读。而今天，我们的生活变得过于丰富了，我想，一个真正不愿意费劲的人一定不会去选择阅读来消遣，他可以有更多简单而直接的事情可做。

a true thinker for himself is spiritually like a monarch. The largest library in disorder is not so useful as a smaller but orderly one; in the same way the greatest amount of knowledge, if it has not been worked out in one's own mind, is of less value than a much smaller amount that has been fully considered.

A man can apply himself of his own free will to reading, while he cannot to thinking. For it is only when a man combines what he knows from all sides, and compares one truth with another, that he completely realizes his own knowledge and gets it into his power. A man can only think over what he knows, therefore he should learn something; but a man only knows what he has pondered.

These might be known to all, but why are they seldom discussed in our times?

It seems that we are busy appealing for more amount of reading, and yet have neglected the quality of it.

However, that is not the case. We are now living in an age different from that of Schopenhauer's, when people did not have many things to do for entertainment, and reading seemed to the only thing left that could be done to kill time without using their brains. Today, our lives have become overly enriched, and a person who does not want to exert much effort will by no means choose reading as a pastime. Anyway, he has more alternatives that are simpler and more straightforward than reading.

也正因为如此，我们不再那么强调在阅读中思考，因为我们知道，在这个时代还愿意阅读的人早就不是那时的人，思考本就融入到我们的阅读中，而我们现在更缺失的是我们丢弃了阅读的时间。

就像叔本华提到的，哪怕是最有智慧的人也不可能一刻不停地思考，而在那些空白时间里，阅读变成了我们积攒能力的时候。叔本华曾呼吁的是那个时代人们的思考，他害怕我们沦为别人思想的奴隶，希望我们能成为自己的思想主人。而现在也许我们更需要的是唤起大家最初始的那份热情，如若不阅读更何谈思考，连基本的沉淀都未曾拥有又怎么追求之后的卓越呢？

It is the very reason why we no longer emphasize the necessity of thinking while reading, for we know that people who are still willing to read books today are not like those in Schopenhauer' era. We have incorporated thinking into our reading from the very beginning. What we need more now is the time for reading.

According to Schopenhauer, even the greatest mind is not always able to think for itself at all times. Therefore, it is advisable for us to use the spare moments in reading to build our abilities. Schopenhauer appealed to people of his times to think for themselves. He hoped that a man can become the master of his own mind and not become a slave of others' thought. At present, what we need to do is to kindle people's original enthusiasm. How could we begin to talk about thinking if we do not read in the first place? How could we expect to achieve excellency if we do not have even

然而阅读始终还是需要思考的。缺乏阅读的我们没有了知识的沉淀，但知识的泛滥却可能会使我们的精神丧失灵敏性，就像是一根弹簧连续不断地受到重压就会推动弹性。如果一个人不想动脑思考，最保险的办法就是一旦空闲了就拿起一本书。这就解释了何以博学多识常使很多人变得比原来更加愚蠢麻木，并阻碍他们的作品获得成功。正如蒲柏所说，他们始终是：不停地阅读别人，却从来不会被别人阅读。因此，单纯的阅读仿佛是积压式的承受，一会儿思考这个，一会儿考虑那个，既非出于本能，亦非因为喜欢。

人总是有惰性的，以前的人不愿意思考，现在的人不愿意阅读，即便阅读了也真的只是在读书而已，这样的知识摄入不仅缓慢而且无效。单纯的经验和阅读一样，并不能取代思考。

有思想之人的作品与其他庸人作品的区别，就在于它主题鲜明、内容明确的特点，及由此而来的清晰、流畅。因为这些人明确、清楚地知道自己想要表达的是什么，不管是以散文、诗歌或者音乐的形式。而普通之人却没有这种果断、清晰，因此二者之间就很容易区分开来。

the minimal accumulation?

Thinking, nevertheless, is always needed while you are reading. If we do not read, we will be short of the accumulation of knowledge; but too much knowledge robs the mind of all elasticity; it is like keeping a spring under a continuous, heavy weight. If a man does not want to think, the safest plan is to take up a book directly he has a spare moment. This practice accounts for the fact that learning makes most men more stupid and dull than they are by nature, and prevents their writings from being a success; they remain, as Alexander Pope has said, "For ever reading, never to be read." The mind thus suffers total compulsion from without; it has first this and first that to think about, for which it has at the time neither instinct nor liking.

Men always have inertia. People in past times were reluctant to think. People in modern age are not willing to read; even when they really read, what they are doing is no more than reading the words in books. It is a slow and ineffective way of taking in knowledge. Mere experience can as little as reading take the place of thought.

The works of all really capable minds are distinguished from all other works by a character of decision and definiteness, and, in consequence, of lucidity and smoothness. This is because minds like these know definitely and clearly what they wish to express — whether it be in prose, in verse, or in music. Other

相信当代的每一位年轻人都不甘平庸，总是希望自己出人头地，但往往只是存在于内心的想法，当实际面对现实时，又会变得茫然。也许每个时代都是一样的，只有每个真正独立思考的人，才能够在精神领域内成为君主。相比之下，那些头脑庸俗的普通大众，随波逐流于各种各样的流行观点、权威说法与世俗偏见之间，使自己的思维受到限制，就像是那些默默服从法律和命令的平民。

说了许久，其实都是后话了，当下我该做的也许还是应该安心的坐下来，认认真真地把我积攒了一年的书籍先消化了，只有走好这第一步，才有可能成为自身的主宰。

阅读，是我们不能遗忘的伙伴；思考，是我们不能停下的步伐。

minds are wanting in this decision and lucidity, and therefore may be instantly recognized.

I believe that all young persons in our era are unwilling to remain mediocre and always wish to be outstanding. But more than often this is only something in their mind; they become at a loss again when facing the real world. The case might be the same throughout the history. Only a true thinker for himself is like a monarch in the realm of mind. On the other hand, those of vulgar minds, who are swayed by all kinds of current opinions, authorities and prejudices, are like the people which in silence obey the law and commands.

What I have said so far is in fact an issue which ought to be discussed later; what I should do at this moment might be to sit down and, with nothing to disturb me, seriously finish all the books piled up in the past year. I cannot become the master of myself before I take this very first step.

Reading is our companion that should not be forgotten, and thinking is our step that should not come to a stop.

沈佳祺
Johnson Shen

所有的相遇，都是久别重逢。不知不觉在CNOOD已经四年多了。在这样一个关怀他人，提升自我的集体中，始终能让自己充满正能量。走遍世界的角落，带着自由而无用的灵魂。

"Every occasion of encounter is a reunion after a long separation. I have been working at CNOOD for more than four years before I know it. I am always filled with positive energy in such a mutually caring and self-promoting organization. With a free and useless soul, I'm going across every corner of the world."

一次印象深刻的发运经历

An Impressive Experience of Shipment

■ David Lee

时间如白驹过隙，转瞬即逝，在施璐德工作年限上，又加上了浓墨重彩的一笔，回顾2018年，有很多感悟和感动，其中令我印象最深刻的经历是扬州的那次发运。

这次发运需要我们协调工厂，在5天内将136支防腐桩管从扬州用3条驳船运至上海，然后直装海轮。因客户未要求按照顺序生产，发运时又规定了不同规格的产品在海轮上的位置，我们需要考虑产品在驳船上的顺序以及3条驳船的直装顺序，时间短、翻倒工作量大、多次装载、天气炎热、工厂无夜班等客观因素，给这次发运增加了很大的协调难度。

Time flies. Another rich and colorful chapter is added to my career at CNOOD. Looking back on the year 2018, I have a myriad of feelings and emotions, with the most impressive experience of the shipment at Yangzhou.

At that time, we needed to coordinate the work done at the manufacturing plant to ensure the transportation of 136 anti-corrosion pipe piles from Yangzhou to Shanghai by three barges in five days before the direct shipment on a ship. The client did not require a sequential production but the positions of products with different specifications on the ship. Therefore, we had to consider the order in which the pipe piles were to be loaded on the three barges as well as the sequence of the direct shipment off the barges. The time limit, heavy workload of, repeated loading, extremely hot weather and the absence of night shift at

为了节约时间，我提前到工厂进行准备。8月29日的早晨，一场大雨把我阻隔在了酒店，直到晌午才停，做了一些防晒工作后就匆匆出发了，午后太阳开始炙烤大地，天气愈发闷热，感觉自己像蒸笼里的扬州包子。没有时间耽搁，我开始在无遮拦的堆场上逐一查对每支桩管的位置，同时，协调相关人员对产品进行油漆修补，重复管号修改，管内杂物清理等工

the plant were all added up together to make it even more difficult to coordinate the work during the shipment.

To save time, I came to the plant ahead of time for preparations. On the morning of August 29, a heavy shower stopped me from leaving the hotel until noon. I left the hotel in a hurry after rubbing some sunscreen into my skin. The earth began to be scorched by the sun while it became sultrier in the afternoon. I felt as if I had been one of

作，并催促有故障的倒运平板车尽快修复。傍晚回到酒店后，发现防晒霜早已被汗水带走，感觉后颈和胳膊火烧般地疼，做了简单的处理后，将统计好的管号整理成电子版，以指导后续工作。第二天，把具体的要求和思路跟工厂交流后，开始装船，一开始按照单独的一支管桩考虑，加上行车需要配合厂内的正常生产，过程断断续续，一天下来只装了12支，按照这个进度肯定不行。第三天，我们改变了思路，按照驳船上的整层来考虑，协调工厂集中整块时间装船，保证过程的连续性，期间，说服工人傍晚加班，并为高温作业环境下工人带去解暑冰品，在工厂、船方的通力配合下，装完了第一条船的剩余部分。后面继续使用之前的方式，又用了两天时间完成两船的装载任务，顺利完成了这次发运。

those Yangzhou stuffed buns in a hot bamboo steamer. Having no time to lose, I started checking the positions of pipe piles one by one at the open container yard. At the same time, I asked the workers to do touch-up painting, amend duplicate pile numbers, and do the in-pipe cleaning, while urging an early repair of the platform truck which had a breakdown. When I went back to the hotel at dusk, I found the sunscreen completely gone with sweat and felt burning aches in my neck and arms. After some simple treatment, I sorted out the pile numbers in an electronic version for reference in the future. The next day, we began the shipment after communicating with the plant about the details. At first, we considered the plan based on every single pile. This idea, together with the driving route designed not to interrupt the normal production schedule in the plant,

made the whole process intermittent, with only twelve piles loaded on the first day. That was simply not good enough if we were to finish the task on time. On the third day, we changed our idea and considered the plan on the basis of a whole layer on the barge. We also asked the plant to use longer periods of time for the loading to ensure the continuity of the process. Meanwhile, we persuaded the workers to work overtime at dusk and prepared ice snacks for them in high-temperature operation. We finished the loading of the remaining cargo of the first barge with the full cooperation of the plant and the shipping company. We spent another two days and completed the loading of the cargo of two barges. The task of shipment was then successfully accomplished.

这次经历，是对我体能和意志力的考验，也让我获得更多的机会去解决问题。在困难面前，我们要利用有限的资源，在充分沟通的基础上，获取更多有用信息，拓宽思路，找到最优解决方案。同时，对公司所倡导的暖文化有了更深的理解，对合作伙伴的充分关心、包容与尊重，可以形成强大的合力，帮助我们顺利完成项目。在此，非常感谢我的团队给予的信任、理解和帮助，成为我强大后盾。

十几天后的9月15日，是我人生中的重要时刻——婚礼，当朋友提到我为什么这么黑时，那一刻，我的内心没有一丝失落，而是满满的获得感，这一切都值得！

The experience is a test of both my physical strength and my willpower. It provides me with more opportunities to solve problems. When facing difficulties, we must, on the basis of sufficient communication, use limited resources and acquire more valuable information and find the optimal solutions with a broad vision. In addition, I have had a deeper understanding of the warm culture proposed by CNOOD. Consideration, tolerance and respect toward our cooperative partners constitute a powerful synergy and help us complete a project successfully. Here I would like to express my gratitude to the trust, understanding and help my team members have given me, which are the strongest backing behind me.

Less than twenty days later, it was September 15, an important moment in my life—my wedding. When I was asked by my friends why I got so tanned, I did not feel the least sense of loss. Instead, I had a sense of full attainment. Everything was worth the effort!

李晓光
David Lee

一个善良、正直的山东烟台人，本科就读于青岛大学高分子材料与工程专业，研究生毕业于复旦大学材料系，爱好书法、运动、读书，希望可以环游世界，非常珍惜并感恩与施璐德结下的缘分，愿与年轻有活力的大家庭共同成长。

A kindhearted, honest person, David Lee is from Yantai, Shandong Province. He graduated from Qingdao University majoring in Polymer Materials Science and Engineering and received his Master's degree at the Department of Materials Science, Fudan University. With hobbies including Chinese calligraphy, sports and reading, he wishes to travel around the world one day. He cherishes and is grateful to the destiny that connects him with CNOOD, hoping to grow together with this young and energetic big family.

不合格报告管理系统开发

Non-Conformance Report Management System Development

■ Lay Tao

摘要：不合格品控制是质量管理工作中的重要环节之一。不合格品的产生实际上是质量活动和过程的失控，其控制会影响到产品对预期要求的符合性以及客户满意度。本文主要通过对 CNOOD ASIA LIMITED 公司现行工作平台中，不合格报告管理系统的开发进行了阐述，并对进一步利用其做好持续改进工作提出了见解。

关键词：不合格报告 质量管理系统 数据 改进

Abstract: The non-conforming product control is one of the key processes in quality management. The occurrence of non-conforming product is actually the mismanagement of quality activities and processes. Its control will affect the conformity of the products to meet the expected requirements and the corresponding customer satisfaction rate. This paper focuses on the introduction of the development of non-conforming report management system in CNOON ASIA LIMITED working platform system and advises on the continuous improvement based on the using of this system.

Key words: non-conforming report, quality management system, data, improvement

1 引言

不合格品控制是企业质量管理工作中

1 Introduction

The non-conforming product

不可或缺的一环，对不符合项的管理反映着企业的质量管理水平并对顾客对企业提供的产品/服务的满意度有很大影响。随着信息技术的不断发展，针对不符合品的控制和管理数据的处理已经可以实现电子化和信息化以提高沟通和处理效率。本文简单介绍了不合格报告管理系统的开发。

2 现行不合格报告处理流程

根据ISO9001 2015的要求，组织应确保对不符合要求的产品和服务得到识别和控制，以防止其非预期的使用和交付对顾客造成不良影响。不合格品的性质以及随后所采取的任何措施的信息应形成文件，包括所批准的让步。

实际在企业的管理中，对于一般的不符合情况，可以根据技术或者质检部门制定的程序进行，但是对于重大的不符合项或不合格品则会制定专门的不合格品的程序，如CNOOD ASIA LIMITED公司（后文简称CNOOD）相应制定了程序文件不合格品的控制（CNOOD-02-008: Control of Non-Conforming Product）。其中，包括了不合格品的识别、不合格品报告的创

control is an indispensable part of a company's quality management. How well a company manages non-conforming items reflects its ability in quality management and exerts great impact on the customer satisfaction of its products and services. With the continued development of information technology, the non-conforming product control and the processing of management data could now be performed by electronic and information-based means in order to promote communication efficiency. This paper focuses on the development of non-conformance reporting management system.

2 The Current Non-Conformance Reporting System Flow

As required by ISO9001 2015, an organization shall ensure that the outputs that do not conform to their requirements are identified and controlled to prevent their unintended use or delivery. The organization shall retain documented information that describes the nature of non-conformity and any action taken, including any concessions approved.

In the actual process of corporate management, ordinary non-conformance could be treated by procedures stipulated by technology or quality control (QC) department. As for major non-conforming items or products, however, specific procedure should be formulated. For example, CNOOD ASIA LIMITED (henceforth CNOOD) has accordingly

建、不合格品的处理、不合格品的纠正措施以及不符合项或产品问题的文件化要求。图1是现行的不符合项/产品的处置流程。

formulated CNOOD-02-008: Control of Non-Conforming Product, which includes the identification of non-conforming product, the creation of non-conformance report, the disposition of non-conforming product, corrective actions for non-conforming product and the documentation requirements of non-conforming items. Fig.1 shows the current non-conforming item management flow.

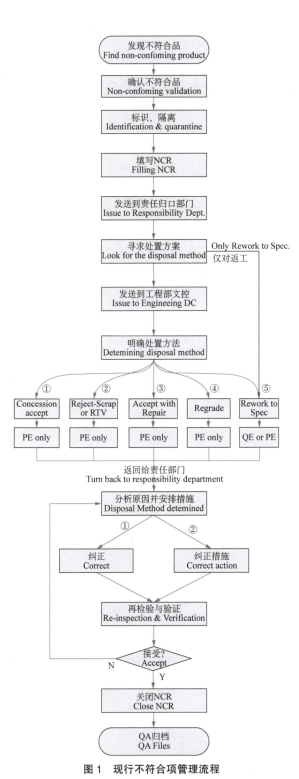

图 1 现行不符合项管理流程
Fig.1　Current Non-Conforming Item Management Flow

由于公司涉及的工程领域比较多元化，在复杂钢结构和工程项目实施过程中，建造的工期相对比较复杂，存在不符合项发生的可能。在质量管理工作中，不合格品控制是一项长期的日常工作。在项目运行过程中，受到各种因素的影响。如何收集这些数据，形成有针对性的改进措施是一项值得研究的课题。根据不符合品控制程序文件现行的不合格报告的处理流程如表 1。

Due to the diversified nature of the engineering fields in which CNOOD is engaged, non-conforming items are likely to occur in implementing complex steel structure and engineering projects with complicated schedules. The non-conforming product control is a long-term task on a daily basis. A project is subject to the influence of various factors. It is a valuable research topic how the data can be gathered to help us work out clearly targeted measures for improvement. The current non-conforming reporting management flow according to non-conforming product control documents is shown in Tab.1.

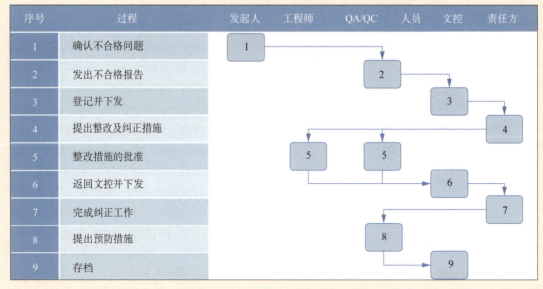

表 1　不合格报告管理流程
Tab.1 Non-conforming Reporting Management Flow

现行的不符合文件管理形式较为传统，依旧是依托于档案管理的模式。无论是文件的传递、保存还是交流过程，都离不开文控人员。CNOOD 质量部在 IT 部门的协助下，开始着手研发自己的不符合报告管理系统。

3　系统设计思路

体系系统是质量赖以形成的有机整体，规范是标准的物化，规范管理是现代企业必备的特质。系统设计以标准依据为前提，以规范、系统化管理为基础，形成良性循环。不符合报告管理系统设计的主要框架建立在不符合项报告的发起、处置、验证、关闭的工作流之上。最终能在系统的载体上分析所有数据。数据是决策的依据，也是持续改进的依据。通过不符合项报告系统的运行，在收集、统计、分析的基础上，充分利用数据改进、提高公司管理体系和生产过程的有效性并最终提高产品质量，才能使不合格品的管理与控制上升一个台阶，并最终提高客户对企业的满意度。

The current non-conforming reporting management adopts a relatively traditional form based on document management. The delivering, saving and exchanging of documents cannot be done without document control clerks. The QC department, with the help from the IT department, sets about developing our own non-conforming reporting management system.

3　The Idea of Systematic Designing

A system is an organic body upon which the quality depends, rules and regulations are the crystallization of standards, and standardized management is indispensable for a modern company. With standards as its prerequisite, systematic designing is based on standardized and systematic management and forms a virtuous circle. The basic framework of the non-conforming reporting management system is built on the work flow of creating, disposing, validating and closing non-conforming reports. Eventually we are able to analyze all the data in the system. Data are the foundation for decision-making as well as for continued improvement. By operating the non-conforming reporting system, we are able, on the basis of data-gathering and statistical analysis, to make full use of the data to make improvement, enhance the effectiveness of the company's management system and production process, and finally improve the quality of products. Only by doing so can we

3.1 不符合项的发起

根据程序，系统做了规定，Non-conforming Report（后文简称NCR）可由CNOOD组织内质量部门的任何人员创建。图2是系统内发起NCR的系统截图，以CNOOD供应商的采购失误为例。

achieve better management and control of non-conforming products, enhancing the customer satisfaction.

3.1 The Creation of Non-conforming Items

It is stipulated in the system that non-conforming report (henceforth referred to as NCR) could be created by any member in the QC department within the organization. Fig.2 is a screenshot showing how an NCR is created in the system, taking a mistake in the purchasing from a supplier as an example.

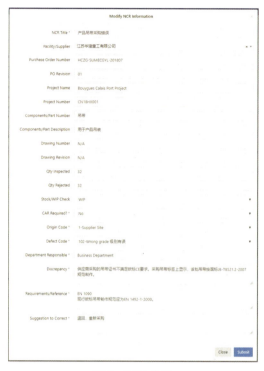

图2　NCR 发起
Fig.2　NCR creation

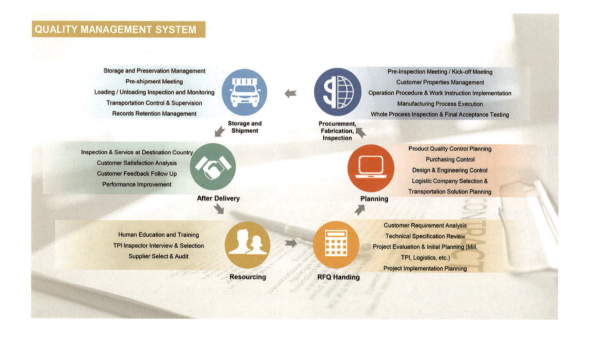

NCR 发起过程，涉及不合格品的识别、不合格报告的创建以及建议纠正措施的提出。其中有部分由系统协助完成的信息，如下：

NCR No.（不符合报告编号）由系统自动编号，以规避可能产生的重号问题。系统内设置的规则是 CNOOD-PI-NCR- 序列号（序列号 = 当天日期 + 当天 NCR 数量统计）。

Date Opened（开具日期），由系统根据创建 NCR 的日期自动填入。

Facility/Supplier（工厂/供应商），填入后系统会将此份 NCR 自动关联到公司供应商管理系统内，作为供应商评价的数据之一。

Project Number（项目编号），填入后系统会将此份 NCR 自动关联到公司项目管理系统内，作为项目管理的数据之一。

Origin Code（来源编码），由系统给出下拉菜单进行选择，有 Supplier Site, Incoming Inspection, Process Inspection, Final Inspection, Storage Inspection, After Delivery，一共六类。为 NCR 问题的来源做了第一级归类（如图 3）。

Defect Code（问题编码），由系统给出下拉菜单进行选择，根据可能产生问题的 17 个方面如材料、设计、机加工、焊接等方面进行第二级归类。并在各大类下进行了问题细分，一共登记了 113 个问题

The process of creating an NCR includes the identification of non-conforming products, the creation of a report and the suggestion of corrective actions. Some of the information is completed with the assistance of the system as follows:

NCR No.: An NCR will be given a number automatically by the system to avoid the case that two NCRs have the same number. The rule set by the system is: CNOOD-PI-NCR-serial number (serial number=date + NCR numbers)

Date Opened: It is entered automatically by the system according to the date when the NCR is created.

Facility/Supplier: After it is entered, an NCR is automatically linked to the management system of suppliers, as one of the factors for supplier evaluation.

Project Number: After it is entered, an NCR is automatically linked to the management system of projects, as one of the factors for project management.

Origin Code: It is determined by selecting one category from the drop-down menu, which includes six categories, i.e. Supplier Site, Incoming Inspection, Process Inspection, Final Inspection, Storage Inspection, and After Delivery. This is the tier-1 classification of the root causes of NCR problems (see Fig.3).

Defect Code: It is determined by selecting one category from the drop-down menu, in which there is a tier-2 classification of seventeen categories including Material, Design, Machining,

编码，对 NCR 进行第三级归类，以便在发生不符合项时，能让系统更精确的对不符合项产生的问题进行登记。系统登记界面如图 4。

Welding, etc. Under these categories we further classify potential problems with a tier-3 classification which includes 113 defect codes, enabling the system to register the root causes of non-conforming items with greater accuracy. The registration interface of the system is shown in Fig.4.

图 3 来源编码
Fig.3 NCR Origin Code

图 4 问题编码
Fig.4 NCR Defect Code

Department Responsible（责任部门），填入后系统会关联到公司的组织架构中设定的部门，进行选择，以确定落实 NCR 处理的责任方。

其他基本信息，如 Purchase Order Number（采购合同号）、PO Revision（采购合同版本号）、Project Name（项目名称）、Drawing Number（图纸编号）等，需 NCR 发起人根据实际情况进行录入。需要特别注意的是 Discrepancy（误差）、Requirements/Reference（要求/参考）、Suggestion to correct（建议纠正措施）需要对质量问题的背景和要求有专业度要求，这也是为何系统内限定了 NCR 发起人必须是公司质量部成员的原因。

在 NCR 起草完成后，可以在下一界面上传 NCR 问题的证明性文件，以便责任方收到 NCR 报告后在系统内进行确认和核实。证明文件可以是任何 office 格式的文件，图片格式或者 PDF 等。NCR 提交完成后的界面如图 5 所示。

3.2 不符合项的处置

不符合项的处置可以是企业内的任何个体。这部分流程的主要工作是对 NCR 产生的根本原因进行分析以及纠正措施的落实。

不合格品原因通常从 5M1E（Man、Machine、Material、Method、Measure、Environment）方面入手查找，查找时可以考虑表 2 中可能存在的原因，一般常用

Department Responsible: It will be linked by the system to a department within the organization to determine the party who is responsible for the disposition of the NCR.

Other basic information, including Purchase Order Number, PO Revision, Project Name, Drawing Number, is entered by the creator of NCR when necessary. Particularly, categories such as Discrepancy, Requirements/Reference and Suggestion to correct have technical requirements as for the background of the quality problems. That is why the creators of NCR are limited to the members of QC department of the company.

After the creation of an NCR, supporting documents are to be submitted on the next interface for the confirmation and validation by the department responsible when the NCR is received. Supporting documents could be in any Office format, JPG or PDF. The interface after the submission of an NCR is shown in Fig.5.

3.2 The Disposition of Non-conforming Items

The disposition of non-conforming items can be performed by any individual member within the company. The main task of this process is to analyze the root causes of NCR and the implementation of corrective actions.

We usually try to find the root causes of the occurrence of non-conforming products from six dimensions, or 5M1E (Man, Machine, Material, Method,

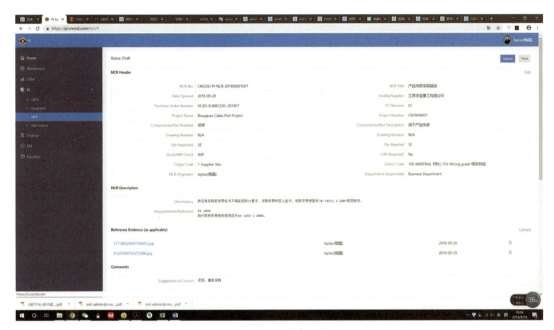

图 5　NCR 发起完成
Fig. 5　NCR Created

表 2　不合格品可能原因汇总表
Tab.2　List of Possible Root Cause of Non-conforming Product

因素	可能涉及的内容
人	操作者不具备相应的资质能力，如：不理解设计图样、不熟悉相关工序规程、不会操作机器、质量意识不强、粗心大意
机	生产中所使用的设备、工具等辅助生产用具不满足要求。如：加工能力不足，机器缺乏维修保养，温湿度等环境条件对设备的影响
料	物料、半成品、配件、原材料等产品用料存在问题。由供应商或组织内部管理不当造成，如材料未经检验或试验、材料混用、代用器材不合格等
法	生产过程中所需要遵循的规章制度（如：工艺指导书、生产图纸、生产计划、产品作业标准、检验标准，各种操作规程等）不完善或未严格执行，以及设计更改未及时贯彻或数控程序编制错误等
环	生产所需的环境不满足要求。如：温湿度、超净间、防静电等不满足要求
测	检测过程存在不足，如：测量设备不符合要求，检验、实验规程含糊不清，检测员不具备相应技能等

的查找原因的方法有现场调查法、头脑风暴法、鱼骨图法、统计分析法等，运用这些质量工具有助于有效而快捷地找出不合格品产生的根本原因。

然后，按照 PDCA 循环的要求，制定相应的纠正措施，如人员素质不符合要求，采取培训学习提高技术能力，调换合格人员等措施；设备过程能力低，则修复、改造、更新设备或作业手段等措施；附属方法问题，则采取改进工艺方法等措施。另外还要注意所采取的纠正措施和不合格影响程度相适应。图 6 是 CNOOD 正在开发的系统内，对纠正措施的记录页面。

在完成纠正措施的记录后，需在系统内上传纠正措施的完成证明，并记录 Disposition Responsible（处置负责人）。不符合项处置完成后系统界面如图 7。（注：展示用案例，故没有证明文件上传在系统内。）

3.3 NCR 处置措施验证

在责任部门相关人员完成 NCR 问题

Measure, Environment). When doing so, we often consider the possible causes as listed in Tab.1 and use tools including on-site survey, brainstorming, fishbone diagram and statistical techniques which help us to identify the root causes of non-conforming products in an effective and convenient way.

Then corrective actions are then taken according to the requirements of PDCA cycle. For example, we carry out training programs to improve technical ability of the personnel or substitute qualified personnel if current personnel are unqualified; we will fix, renovate and update the facilities or operational means if their capacity fail to reach the required standard; we try to improve the technological methods if there is any problem in them. In addition, make sure that the corrective actions are proportional to the extent of non-conformance. Fig. 6 shows how corrective actions are recorded in a system being developed.

After a corrective action is recorded, a validation document is submitted in the system while the Disposition Responsible (one who is responsible for the disposition) is recorded. The system interface after the disposition of a non-conforming item is shown in Fig. 7. (No validation document is submitted in the system for the purpose of demonstration.)

3.3 The Verification of NCR Disposition

When the corrective actions are

图 6 纠正措施记录
Fig. 6 Corrective Action Record

图 7 处置完成
Fig. 7 Disposition Completed

的纠正措施并提交后，由公司 QA/QC 人员对纠正措施进行验证。其验证操作界面如图 8。

处置措施验证过程中，QA/QC 人员需对验证的措施进行记录和最终判定。并负责对不符合品的修复品进行再检验，同时对相关措施的实施与否及其有效性进行验证，其中：

Validation Comment（验证意见）由 QA/QC 人员在对处置责任人的处置完成并确认后根据结果进行填写。

Disposition Type（处置类型），根据程序文件由系统给出下拉菜单进行选择，包括：Concessive Acceptance（让步接收）、Rework（返工）、Repair（返修）、

taken and submitted, they will be further validated by QA/QC of the company. The interface of the validation of disposition is shown in Fig. 8.

During the validation of disposition, QA/QC is required to record the corrective actions and make final judgment, who is also responsible for re-examining the restored one of a non-conforming product, while validating the implementation of corresponding measures and their effectiveness.

"Validation Comment" is written by QA/QC after the disposition is completed and confirmed.

"Disposition Type" is determined by selecting an item form a drop-down menu, which includes Concessive Acceptance, Rework, Repair, Degrade,

图 8　处置措施验证
Fig. 8　Validation of Disposition

Degrade（降级使用）、Reject/Return to Vendor /Scrap（拒收 / 退回供应商 / 报废）。

Re-inspected by（复检人）、Reinspection Result（复检结果）Disposition Qty（处置数量）、Disposition Description（处置描述）根据 NCR 处置的情况进行记录。

若 NCR 经过 QA/QC 人员验证不能关闭，则在系统内将 NCR 退回责任部门进行再处理。

3.4　NCR 的关闭

NCR 经过 QA/QC 人员验证可以关闭，则在系统内确认后进行关闭。其 NCR 状态可以在系统自动生成的汇总目录内确认，并根据 NCR 编号、NCR 名称、NCR 状态进行快速检索。如图 9。

Reject/Return to Vendor /Scrap.

"Re-inspected by", "Reinspection Result", "Disposition Qty" and "Disposition Description" are recorded according to the disposition of NCR.

If an NCR cannot be closed after the validation by QA/QC, it is then returned to the department responsible for re-disposition.

3.4　The Closing of NCR

An NCR can be closed after the validation by QA/QC. This is done in the system after validation. The state of the NCR can be confirmed in the general catalogue created automatically by the

图 9 NCR 汇总
Fig. 9 NCR Summary

system, and can be searched by NCR No., NCR name and NCR state in a convenient way.

4 数据统计和分析功能展望

不合格品控制的意义不仅仅是对现在不合格品的处理,更重要的是预防。要想对不合格品进行有效预防,就需要在现有不合格基础上,汇总、分析原因,为消除产生不合格品的原因和潜在不合格品的原因,提供充分的证据,把质量管理工作的重点从事后把关转移到对不合格品的再发生事前控制,切实提高产品的实物质量。

4 Data Statistics and Analysis Functions

The control of non-conforming products is meaningful not only because it deals with the current non-conforming products but also because it helps prevent the occurrence of them. An effective prevention of the occurrence of non-conforming products requires the summary and analysis of the root causes on the basis of current non-conformance and provides sufficient proof for eliminating the root causes of current and potential non-conformance. It focuses on the before-the-event control of non-conformance instead of the after-the-event check and greatly enhancing the quality of our products.

目前 CNOOD 公司的不合格报告管理系统，尚在初级开发阶段，系统已经开始收集数据但尚未完成数据统计和汇总并提供分析结论的功能，并不能提供类似图 10 进行的 NCR 数据分析能力。相信在不久的将来，该系统会帮助企业在提高质量管理方面提供高效、有效的支持。

The current non-conforming reporting management system is in its early stage of development. It has begun to gather data and yet is not able to perform such functions as data summarization and statistical analysis. The NCR analytical ability as demonstrated in Fig. 10 is yet to be developed. The system is believed, in the near future, to provide the company with highly efficient, effective support in enhancing its quality management.

5 总结

一直以来，质量信息统计和数据分析工作都是企业质量管理的薄弱环节，其中原因之一是由于产品种类多，数量少，难以形成足够的数据源。那不妨就从不合格品统计方面入手，对本企业一段时期内产生的不合格品进行系统梳理，全方位总结分析，一定能发现有价值的信息和规律，找到解决问题的突破口。这也是 ISO 9001 2015 标准中对企业的要求。通过此 NCR

5 A Summary

The quality information statistics with data analysis has long been a weak link in corporate management. One of the reasons for this is that we do not have a data source big enough because of the varicty of products and their small quantity. By starting from the statistics of non-conforming products and conducting a systematic, comprehensive analysis

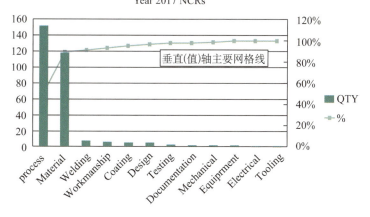

306 NCRs issued in year 2017.
Top two defecr code:Process,Material

图 10　Non-conformance 分析
Fig. 10　Non-conformance Analysis

报告管理系统的建立，能帮助企业对不合格品统计进行数据分析，增加所获得数据的增值。帮助企业挖掘在设计、生产、工艺、操作、质量管理等方面存在的深层次不足和薄弱环节，找准关键因素防控点，提出改进措施，抓好落实，努力构建以预防为主的管理体系和长效机制，促进企业产品质量以及客户满意度的不断提高。

of the non-conforming products of the company during a certain period of time, we are sure to find valuable information and the breakthrough point for solving problems. This is exactly the requirement for a company in ISO 9001 2015. Our NCR management system helps the company to carry out statistical analysis of non-conforming products and increase the value-added of the data acquired. It helps the company explore the deeply rooted shortcomings and weak points in its designing, manufacturing, technology, operations and quality management, while precisely identifying prevention and control points as for key factors. By offering suggestions of improvement measures, it helps the company do a good job of implementation and build a prevention-based management system and mechanism with a long-lasting effect, continuously improving the product quality and customer satisfaction.

参考文献：

[1] The International Organization for Standardization. Quality management systems—Requirements: ISO 9001 2015[S] Fifth edition.

[2] 黄仁贵，张忠诚. 海洋工程施工中不合格品控制 [J]. 中国造船, 2007.

[3] 王辉，龚莉莉，果长悦，陈涛，王喀生. 科研所不合格品控制要求案例分析探究 [J]. 中国科学院声学研究所，2016(4). DOI:10.13237/j.cnki.asq.2016.04.010.

[4] 郭元明. 浅谈不合格品控制及质量事故处理方法 [J]. 建筑工程技术与设计, 2016(4).

Bibliography:

[1] The International Organization for Standardization. Quality management systems — Requirements: ISO 9001 2015 [S] Fifth edition.

[2] HUANG Rengui, ZHANG Zhongcheng. Non-conforming product control in offshore project construction [J]. China Shipping, 2007.

[3] WANG Hui, GONG Lili, GUO Changyue, CHEN Tao, WANG Kasheng. Case study on the control requirements of non-conforming products in scientific research institutes [J]. China academy of sciences the institute of acoustics, 2016(4). DOI:10.13237/j.cnki.asq.2016.04.010.

[4] GUO Yuanming. Talking about the control method of non-conforming product and the handling method of quality accident[J]. Construction engineering technology and design, 2016(4).

陶 磊
Lay Tao

1986 年 2 月出生于上海。毕业于上海工程技术大学，目前上海同济大学 MBA 在读。曾在大型跨国国企以及知名外资公司任关键职位。对项目管理和质量控制有丰富经验。

Lay Tao was born in Shanghai in February 1986. Graduating from Shanghai University of Engineering Science, he is now an MBA student at Tongji University. He held key positions in large transnational state-owned enterprises and famous foreign companies, with rich experience in project management and quality control.

生活这件"小"事

Life Is But a "Small" Case

■ Jane Yan

戊狗迎亥猪 转眼又是一年。

去年春节的一幕幕还在眼前，转眼便又是一个除夕夜。长大后，"年"彷佛踏上了风火轮，跑得特别快。

2018 年，我经历了许多细碎微小的幸福，也面临了许多艰难的时刻和跌宕起伏。一年到头回头看，还是挺感慨的。人类，真的是很顽强啊！你总能比自己想象中更努力一点，承受的东西也更多一点……

我曾经误以为，人是要活成别人想要的样子、符合别人的期待才算成功，因此陷入了一个怪圈，不断努力希望得到他人的认可，得不到就会认为自己不够好，不

The year of the Dog is, before I notice it, coming to an end. We are ushering in the year of the Boar.

We are about to celebrate another Lunar New Year's Eve when the scenes of last year's Spring Festival are still fresh in my memory. Times seem to pass extremely fast when we are no longer kids.

In 2018, I experienced many little doses of happiness while facing many hard times and turbulences. Looking back at the end of the year, I am filled with a myriad of emotions. Human beings are really tough creatures. You always work harder than you imagine and are able to take on more burdens than you think you could.

I used to think that we are successful only if we to live in the way expected by others. Therefore, I seemed to have fallen into a vicious circle: I worked hard

自信。然而，依靠他人获得幸福感和安全感的方式是十分不稳定的，于是就会不断的自我否定，徒增烦恼。

直到有一天，许久不见的老朋友打来电话，第一句就是问最近过的好不。那一刻我突然也想问自己：我是否事业顺利，关系圆满？是否婚姻幸福，家庭和谐？是否喜悦快乐，身心健康？自问之后，我很惭愧地意识到，有很多方面，我做得还不够好。而且我惊讶地发现，这些围绕着我的，都只跟我自己本身有关。所以，我只有把自己做好，淋漓尽致地发挥智慧、爱心和决心，并为之投入百分之百的努力，生活才能幸福圆满。不是吗?!

incessantly in order to be accepted by others; if not, I would not regard myself good enough and become unconfident. However, it is unsteady to try to get your happiness and the sense of security by other people; you begin to deny yourself and become anxious for no reason.

Things went on until one day, an old friend who had not seen me for a long time called me and asked how I was doing recently. At that very moment I too wanted to ask myself: "Am I successful in my career and personal relations? Am I happy in my marriage and family? Do I enjoy life? Am I healthy both physically and mentally?" After asking myself these questions, I was sorry to be aware that I did not do a good job in many aspects. And it was to my surprise that these problems around me had nothing to do with anyone else. That is to say, I could have a happy, perfect life only if I become a better person, give full play to my wisdom, love and determination and work hard to the best of my abilities. Isn't that the case?

瞬间感觉像被闪电击中。

原来，只有当你开始关注自身，回归内在，才能够帮助自己照顾好自己，千万别因为太想周全不想出错而活在别人的眼光里，最后却活成了自己最不喜欢的样子。而且人啊，别总是给自己太多的束缚，其实有时候忘记痛苦，不要比较，别怕失去，永远记得当年许下梦想的自己，那个心里有热血、眼里有光芒的自己，勇敢的朝梦想迈步，人生才有可能改变。无论这一步是否糟糕，不要计较不要回头，相信自己只要努力去做，总能到达想要去的地方。

随着年龄渐长，和社会的交集越来越多，也越来越体会到，我并不完美，总会有一些事没做好，或者不如意，这都是正常的，并不需要过度责怪自己，不要让过高的自我要求阻碍对自我优点的认知，也不要活在过往里，跟旧时光缠斗。认认真真活好当下，拥有独立的思想，能够照顾他人的情绪，清楚自己的尺度和边界，深谙自己的天赋所在，既有想要爆发的欲望，也笃定不会失控，知世故而不世故，自尊自爱、张弛有度，我想，这才是最好的自己。

All of a sudden, I felt as if I had been struck by a lightning.

It turns out that you are able to look after yourself only if you begin to pay attention to yourself and return to the inside. Never try to live in other people's eyes just because you wish to be a perfect, faultless person, or you will end up in being a person you dislike the most. Don't impose too many restrictions on yourself. In fact, you can make a difference in your life if you forget the pains and the comparison, fear not to lose anything, remember forever your dreams, passion and hope, and bravely stride forward to achieve your dreams. Don't be too calculating nor turn back whether it will be a bad situation. Believe you can always be where you wish to if you work hard for it.

When I grow older, I have more and more connections with the world and become increasingly aware that I am not a perfect person and there will always be things I can not do well. It is just quite normal. There is no need to blame myself. Never stop to find your merits because of too high a self-requirement, nor live in the past and be entangled with the old days. Live a worthy life for the present moment. Think independently. Show consideration for others. Know where your limitations and boundaries lie and what your talents are. Have a desire to burst, and yet make sure you do not lose control. Know the worldly business, while avoid being a worldly person.

古训讲：修身齐家治国平天下。修身放在首位可见其重要性。修身三修：修心，修性，修行。只有自己足够强大，才能正确面对生活中的种种不如意，能选择，懂放弃，懂得尽人事，听天命，不贪婪，不妄求，懂宽容，知进退，宠辱不惊，成功了不洋洋自得，失败了不悲观失意，在忙碌之中体会内心的宁静和生活的乐趣，从而真正做自己的主人。

一辈子太短，做自己喜欢的事，读自己喜欢的书，越来越接近自己喜欢的样子，很难，但很重要。

一年又一年，每个人都在收获成长。所谓成长，就是逼着你一个人，跟跟跄跄受伤，跌跌撞撞地坚强。

产假之后的相当长一段时间里，一直在努力处理自己的新身份所带来的一系

Maintain self-respect. Know when to go and when to stop. This is, it seems to me, the way to be your best self.

The old teaching says, "A true gentleman should cultivate his person, regulate his family, rightly govern his state, and then the world will be given peace." We can see the importance of self-cultivation because it is put in the first place. Self-cultivation includes three things: the cultivation of your heart, of your nature and of your conduct. You are able to take a correct attitude toward all the adversities in life only if you are strong enough. You are your own master if you know what to choose and when to give up, do all that is humanly possible while leaving the rest to God, restrain yourself being greedy and making unwarranted demand, learn to be tolerant, know when to advance and when to retreat, keep your head cool whether bestowed with favor or subjected to humiliation, never be carried away by success nor be upset by failure, and try to feel the inner tranquility and the delights of life.

Life is short. It is hard and yet important to do things you like, read books you like, and become infinitely closer to the way you like.

Year after year, everyone has been growing. When you grow, you get injured and yet become stronger while staggering along all by yourself.

In quite a long time after my maternity leave, I was trying hard to cope

列改变，带娃琐事、陡增的开支和长期睡眠不足，导致体力和精力消耗极大，情绪变得很紧张；另一方面，回来上班之后也不太适应从工作满满到突然闲下来的这种落差，而且感觉专注力和记忆力都有所下降，熟悉的工作找不到以前游刃有余的感觉，同时还需要尽快学习新知识跟得上公司的发展变化，有一种前所未有的无力感和紧迫感；长时间的空档期，和同事的沟通也出现了困难，大家讨论的话题很多也不熟悉；当看着儿子一天天长大，又会产生莫名的负罪感，因为自己很少时间陪他……这好几重压力一度令我心慌焦虑得很，那种感觉我想只有经历过的人才会懂。久而久之，工作和家庭都没能做得好，结果心理压力更大了。更糟糕的是这些情绪根本没时间消化，尝试过跟朋友同事倾诉，但是大家要么很忙要么也不能完全理解，反而因为自己的情绪影响了别人。所以后来就不自觉地就把自己封闭起来，只想自己慢慢调整悄悄自愈。

with the changes brought by my new identity. On one hand, because of the chores in looking after my baby and the quickly increasing expenses and constant lack of sleep, I was consuming too much of my strength and energy these days, causing a considerable mental tension. On the other, I was not used to the big gap between a busy working schedule to a sudden relax, with a decline in my attention and memory. I was not able to work as effortlessly as I used to. At the same time, I had to learn new knowledge as soon as possible to catch up with the fast-growing company. I felt a sense of powerlessness and urgency stronger than ever. After a long period without working, I found it a little difficult to communicate with my colleagues who talked about things with which I was unfamiliar. Meanwhile, I would feel inexplicably guilty to see my baby son growing up day by day while I hardly have enough time to be with him... I became extremely anxious under these manifold pressures which could be understood only by those who had personally experienced them. As a result, I did not do a good job in either work or family, leading to an even greater mental stress. To make things worse, I did not have the time to handle the stress. I tried to talk to my friends or colleagues, but they were too busy to listen or just couldn't understand what I was saying. I was afraid that they too were affected by my negative emotions. Unwittingly I began to lock myself up, hoping to heal

　　庆幸的是，有老池的敏锐，让这段对我来说异常艰难的时间没有持续更长。他以洞悉一切的、一个过来人的、一个可信赖的长者的身份，语重心长的点醒我：别着急，慢慢来。

　　不适应就慢慢适应，宽容对待所有的变化。

　　除了自身客观条件的不允许，社会普遍认为刚生完小孩的女性全部心思都在孩子上，一般也不敢委以重任，这确实令人很失落。但换一个角度来想，这也是正常的，而且抚育小孩原本也需要大量精力和

myself by gradual self-adjustment.

　　Luckily, the extremely difficult period of time for me did not last long, thanks to the penetrating observation of Dennis. As a reliable veteran who has an insight into everything, he awakens me by saying, "Don't hurry! Take your time."

　　Try to adapt slowly if you find it hard to do so. Embrace all the changes with an open mind.

　　In addition to their own conditions, female workers who have just had babies are generally believed to put in their energy in child-rearing and therefore will not be given important tasks. This is really

时间，多一点时间陪陪，孩子一晃眼就长大了，毕竟第一次坐，第一次爬，第一次走路，第一次牙牙学语，过去了就永远不会再回来。而且周围的同事小伙伴儿们在工作上也一直对我特别理解和照顾，给了我足够的时间和空间来过渡。

想通了这些，心头的雾霾便消散了很多。

于是我努力调整心态，工作上开始重新系统学习 CAD、SolidWorks 等工程软件和 Office 办公软件，通过提高工作效率来做到事半功倍，加强英语的复习和学习，同时关心行业趋势并针对性地阅读相关的专业书籍……我相信，只有先把自己武装好，才能更好地投入下面的工作。

生活上也结交了一些职场妈咪做朋友，和她们多聊天，互相鼓励，也尽可能挤出一点时间给自己，即使是一个热水澡，或是一首歌的时间，心情真的会变好。心情好了，和孩子相处时才能全心全意感染给他快乐。我也慢慢地认识到，带孩子是很苦很累，但孩子也教会了我很多东西，我不是一个完美的妈妈，但我会一直努力去做。

disappointing. However, if we look at it from a different angle, we will consider it as a normal phenomenon. Besides, child-rearing requires for the first place a lot of energy and time. Parents should pay more time to be with their little babies, who will grow up before you know it. The times when your babies are able to sit, crawl, walk and talk take place only once. And my colleagues around me show particular understanding and care to me at work, giving me ample time and space to finish the transformation.

My mind becomes clear when I have thought it through.

Therefore, I try hard to adjust my frame of mind and begin to learn again engineering software such as CAD and SolidWorks and the Microsoft Office, trying to achieve maximum results by minimum effort. I make intense effort in English learning and revision. At the same time, I pay a lot of attention to business trends and read professional books in relevant fields...I can do a better job in my work in the coming days, I believe, only if I am fully prepared.

I have made friends with a number of working moms. I have frequent conversations with them while encouraging each other. I try to find time for myself, even so short a period as to have a hot bath or listen to a song. This really makes me feel happier. And I can deliver happiness to my kid whole-heartedly only when I am happy myself. Slowly I am aware that it is a demanding

其实，每一个人在生命的某一个阶段，都会有段特别艰难的时候，可是，当这件事情有一天终于过去，你回过头来再看看那段过往，发现不过如此。虽然在一些特别特别难过的时刻，你也会期待来自他人的鼓励，哪怕是一点点，也许都会让你的心情好过一点，可是最终，你都靠自己挺过来了。那些当时难熬的时光，终将过去，唯一留下的是经历，是成长。

此后，你将一身荣光，风雨不惧。

我们都是正在编织梦想的普通人，生活中苦辣酸甜交织，欢乐苦难并存，也常常上一秒自己打鸡血，下一秒被现实泼冷水。很戳心，是不是？可我们的生活不就是这样的吗，活成什么样子就看你有没有为自己的梦想努力，被打击之后是否还保持初心，要知道，努力不是可耻的事，投降才是，逃避才是。那些杀不死我们的，都能使我们更强大。

无论何时，活出属于自己的风华和姿态。

task to look after a baby, but I am also taught many new things by my kid. I am not a perfect mom, but I will go on and try to be one.

In fact, everyone will have an extremely hard time in some stage of his/her life. However, you will find it no more than an ordinary case when you look back on it when it is over one day. When you were at extremely depressed hours, you would expect to be encouraged by others and would invariably feel better no matter how tiny the encouragement was. However, you always braved it out by yourself. Those hard hours would be history one day, and what would be left are your experience and growth.

From then on, you will be courageous enough to face all the adversities with honor.

We are all common dream-weavers, who taste both the sweetness and bitterness of life. We are often pumped up by ourselves at one moment and discouraged by the reality the next moment. Very disappointing, isn't it? However, this is exactly what life is about. The type of life you will have depends on whether you have worked hard for your dream and whether you remain true to your original aspiration after being discouraged. Remember: To work hard is not a shame, but to give yourself up and to escape are. We are made stronger by whatever cannot destroy us.

Always be yourself with your own elegance and attitude.

无论何时，多给自己一些快乐，温暖、力量和勇气。

无论何时，仍怀揣一颗炙热的心，永远在路上。

你看前面，阳光灿烂。

Always give some joy, warmth, strength and courage to yourself.

Always be passionate on a journey to which there is no end.

Look ahead, and you will see the bright sunlight.

闫京亚
Jane Yan

毕业于上海大学机械工程专业，2014 年 7 月加入施璐德。感性工科女，靠谱金牛座。认真工作，热爱生活。愿用无比真诚和不断向上的初心与这个特别的集体共振。

Jane graduated from Shanghai University majoring in Mechanical Engineering, and joined CNOOD in July 2014. She is at once a sentimental female engineer and a dependable Taurus. She works hard and loves life. She wishes to resonate with the unique organization by her usual sincerity and original aspiration of making continuous progress.

曼德勒市市长耶伦博士到访施璐德 EPC 项目现场

Mandalay Mayor Dr. Ye Lwin Visit CNOOD EPC Project Site

■ Jackie Chen, Amanda Wu & Rocky Yuan

MYWW 3.0 项目背景：曼德勒市 Shwege 洪涝泵房及配套建设 EPC 项目，业主为曼德勒市政发展委员会。合资成员包括：施璐德亚洲有限公司；中国能源建设集团湖南省电力设计院。

2019 年 1 月 10 日，MYWW3.0 项目部迎来了曼德勒市政府的首次视察，到访的有曼德勒市市长耶伦博士及 11 名市政委员会成员，陪同前来的还有业主单位项目管理办公室的 30 名工作人员及媒体记者。

MYWW 3.0 Project Background: Mandalay Shwege Stormwater Pumping Station and Substation EPC project, the employer is Mandalay City Development Committee.

JV member: CNOOD ASIA LIMITED, CEEC-HEPDI.

On January 10, 2019, the MYWW3.0 project department ushered the first inspection of Mandalay municipal government, Mayor Dr. Ye Lwin and 11 committee members, accompanied by 30 persons from PMO of employer Mandalay City Development Committee and media journalists.

施璐德亚洲有限公司董事长池勇海先生、常务副董事长袁红庆先生获悉曼德勒市政府即将来访后，随即调整行程，于1月10日凌晨3时抵达项目现场，以便能够按时出席相关会议，为公司在缅EPC业务发展打下坚实基础。

首先，在项目现场，项目负责人陈淙洁先生向市长汇报了项目现场的临时建筑施工进度以及后续计划，提出在5月雨季到来之前完成市政工程的建设。

Chairman Mr. Dennis Chi and Executive Vice President Mr. Guyer Yuan arrived at project site at 3 am on January 10 immediately after hearing the Mandalay government visiting news, they adjusted itinerary to attend the meeting on time, laying a solid foundation for EPC development in Myanmar.

Firstly, at the project site, project representative Jackie Chen reported to the mayor, based on the temporary construction and construction progress of the project site, as well as later planning, proposed to complete the civil works before the rainy season in May.

VISION DRIVEN LIFE-CNOOD 2008 TO 2018

随后，双方在项目现场的会议室举行了正式会晤。陈淙洁先生代表施璐德亚洲有限公司和中国能源建设集团湖南省电力设计院，就项目的具体细节做了汇报。袁红庆先生分析了碎石桩的技术要点，其中，碎石料借助转角的自锁效应而紧密胶结。同时，我们与督导科林·莱格先生就技术问题展开了深入的交流。耶伦博士也展现出了很高的专业素养和极大的兴趣，并提议日后前来参观碎石桩的相关测试。

耶伦博士高度评价了我方的工作。拍摄集体照之后，池勇海先生、袁红庆与耶伦博士进行了亲切交谈；结束后，二人欢送曼德勒市政府成员经由临时安全通道离开。

耶伦博士也在脸书上分享了此次访问。

Subsequently, we held a formal meeting in site conference room. Jackie Chen represented CNOOD&CEEC-HEPDI and reported the specific details of project. Mr. Guyer Yuan analysed technical essential of stone column. The stone is closely combined by the self-locking effect of the corners. At the same time developed technical exchange with supervision Mr. Colin Legg deeply. Also Dr. Ye Lwin was very professional and interested, proposed to witness stone column test later.

Dr. Ye Lwin spoke highly of our work. After taking group photo, Mr. Dennis Chi & Guyer Yuan had a cordial conversation with Dr. Ye Lwin and saw off Mandalay municipal government through temporary secure channel.

Dr. Ye Lwin also highlighted this visiting in Facebook.

陈淙洁
Jackie Chen

东华大学物理化学硕士。我喜欢去林间思索。这里有花香,有虫鸣。一阵风来,吹过树叶,所有的问题便都有了答案——傻傻傻傻傻傻……

Jackie graduated from Donghxua University as Master of Science in Physical Chemistry. "I like to meditate in the forest, where there is the fragrance of flowers and the chirping of insects. I find the answer to all the questions with the sound of tree leaves rustling in the wind: silly, silly, silly…"

邬 成
Amanda Wu

邬成,2016年硕士毕业于上海大学材料科学学院,外表柔弱,内心强大,不认怂。

Amanda graduated from School of Materials and Science & Engineering, Shanghai University with a Master's degree in 2016. With a delicate and meek appearance, she has a strong heart and never shrinks back.

袁乐南
Rocky Yuan

在山东,玩耍过童年,也完成了义务教育,大学辗转到重庆,看了看中国另外一角,而后硕士,踏上英国的飞机,看了看世界另外一角。机缘之中遇到CNOOD,包罗万物,没有边界,元气满满。心怀希翼,还在征途。

At his hometown in Shandong Province, Rocky Yuan spent his childhood playing and completed the compulsory schooling as well. He went to university in Chongqing after passing through many different places and saw another corner of China, before he flied to UK for pursuing a Master's degree and saw another corner of the world. By destiny he encountered CNOOD, all-embracing, borderless, and brimming with life. With hope in his mind, he is still on the journey.

实习小结

Internship Summary

■ Zhou Chuang

尊敬的池总：

您好，我是周创。首先非常感谢您能提供给我这次宝贵的实习机会，短短的一个月对我却是一段十分充实美好的回忆。除去以前高中的职业生涯体验和大学里作为助教的兼职，这也如是我初出茅庐，第一次踏入社会真正意义上的实习。在怀揣着"把酒御前听秋雨"的憧憬和"少年不识愁滋味"的踟蹰中伊始。

初来乍到最大的体验就是单位同事的热情和朝气。丹妮姐非常热情地给我做了公司的基本介绍和项目领域，环视一圈发现附近的同事也都是年轻的面孔，这个以90后为主力军的企业着实让我眼前一亮，感叹您敢用新人的同时也不禁扪心自问几年后的自己是否也能像在座的学长学姐一样能够落落大方地为人处事，独当一面。

My dear Mr. Chi:

My name is Zhou Chuang. First of all, I am very grateful to you for this valuable opportunity of internship you have given me. For me, the short period of one month is a rich, beautiful memory. Apart from the job experience during high school and the part-time work as TA at university, the internship marks my first step into society. With longings for "listening to the autumn rain with wine" and the hesitation typical of "youth that knows no sorrow", I began my journey at CNOOD.

The enthusiasm and youthful vitality of the colleagues at CNOOD were the things that impressed me the most when I was newly arrived. Danni warmly gave me a brief introduction about CNOOD and its project fields. Looking around me, I found most of my colleagues to be young people. I was greatly excited when I

　　另一个非常惊喜的发现就是公司的国际化程度之高，大家共处一室，为了共同的项目目标努力，这样的公司凝聚力确实很让人羡慕。

knew that people born in the 90s formed the mainstay of the company. While I was deeply moved by your courage to choose new employees, I couldn't help asking myself whether I, in several years, would be able to behave naturally and gracefully and to cope with my job all on my own, just as the senior members in the company did.

　　I was also amazed by how highly international CNOOD is. Leaders from various countries, worked together under the same roof for the same goal of a project. This is a kind of corporate

回顾一下这一个月来所做的事情，虽然没有直接接触项目投标内容，但通过与项目合作公司的文件翻译（建筑手册，投标公司项目介绍，洋麻项目准备工作的翻译）过程中还是了解到了许多招标、竞标的流程及企划方案。洋麻造纸项目是这次实习最主要的工作内容，前期配合丹妮姐为赴哈萨克斯坦交流的农业专家制作宣讲用PPT，搜查关于洋麻造纸可行性的资料，期间运用之前在国外一直使用的infographic在线编辑器制作了一份关于纸业的图像宣传册，之后便开始了关于洋麻造纸行业较为专业的行业报告的撰写。这份40页的报告书也是我第一次尝试撰写行业分析报告，总结了洋麻的特性、种植环境、国内外造纸行业的现状及供求关系、哈萨克斯坦相关的种植条件及政策和造纸的生产工序等等，整条逻辑下来由于行业背景知识的不足和市场价格的不了解，报告内容还是稍显粗糙，不过最大的收获是了解到了行业报告撰写的格式和内容要求。后来从丹尼那里听来的反馈，专家的谈判也比较顺利，试种的洋麻种子也陆续发芽，发回的报告中也提到哈方同样非常看重洋麻造纸的项目，这几日也正在安排来华进行商务访问，进一步落实项目的规划并且确定从滴灌到纸浆厂生产各个环节的具体相关事宜。已经递交他们的出访邀请函，希望他们能够顺利拿到签证，整个项目早一些实现开工。

cohesiveness that would be the envy of the world.

　　When I recall what I did in the past month, I find that though I was not directly involved in project bidding I still learned a lot about its process and planning program through the translation of the documents provided by our partner companies (architecture manual, project profile of the bidding company, preparatory work of the kenaf project). My work during the internship was focused on the kenaf-based papermaking project. In the initial stage, I assisted Danni in preparing PowerPoint presentations for agricultural experts who were going to Kazakhstan to communicate regarding the project, and collecting data concerning the feasibility of kenaf-based papermaking, during which time I prepared an illustrated brochure about the paper industry using the on-line editor "infographic". After that I began to write the professional industry report of kenaf-based papermaking. The 40-page report was my first attempt at industry analysis, in which I summarized the specific attributes and growing environment of kenaf, the current situation of papermaking industry and the market conditions both at home and abroad, the growing conditions and relevant policies in Kazakhstan, and the manufacturing process of paper. Because of my insufficient knowledge of the industry and market price, the report appeared a little crude. My greatest gain

其他几次去工商局改注册地址，参加单位会议，接见客户等工作也都让我丰富了眼界，了解了正在运转的商业模式，除此之外，想更多地谈一谈我感受到的单位企业氛围。时至今日，触动我最深的是这里良好的同事氛围，未曾走进社会的我即使不相信极端少见的职场中的尔虞我诈，你死我活，却也或多或少了解商业环境较之校园环境要来得复杂，但是这为期一个月的实习让我收获的更多的是互助的友谊和感动。虽未曾有机会对比过其他老板的为人处事，但至少您带出的这支队伍绝非传统印象中职场那般的刻薄。记得听我爸说过您读书人出身的经历让您更符合一位"儒商"的形象，亲身感受过还是能体会到不一样的团队氛围和公司精神。最怀念的是每天中午单位集体出去吃中饭的情景，饭桌上轻松的话题，树荫下并排的背

from it, however, was that I learned the requirement for writing an industry report, including the form and content. Later, according to the feedback from Danni, the negotiation went quite smooth and the experimental seeds of kenaf put forth sprouts one after another. It was mentioned in the report from Kazakhstan that they were also very interested in the project, and were arranging for business visit to China to further put into implementation the planning of the project and fix all issues from drip irrigation to manufacturing details in the pulp mill. We have submitted their invitation letter, hoping that they would be able to get the visa successfully and that the project could start as soon as possible.

In addition, several things I took part in, including altering the company's registration address at the Administration for Industry and Commerce, attending business conferences at the company, and meeting with our clients, have broadened my horizon and given me a better understanding of the way we run business. Apart from that, I would like to talk more about the corporate atmosphere of CNOOD I have felt. Before I stepped into society, I knew more or less that the business environment is far more complicated than campus life though I did not believe in the extreme case of mutual deception or life-and-death strife within an organization. But during the one-month internship, what I

影似乎感觉这更像是高中时代一个清澈纯真的午休下午。从学长学姐那里听来的实习经历，多是气氛的凝重和僵硬，接触的所有单位没有一家能够像我们一样坦诚地坐在一张饭桌前共进午餐，说实话在我眼里这样生活化的场景远胜许多"有名无实"的公司团建。也许我现在的所见还很浅显，也不知日后的自己是否会被社会改得急功近利，但至少多年以后回想起这段经历，我还是会第一反应跳出那个静谧的夏天的中午。

想说却还没说的还很多，千言万语还是化作一句谢谢，非常感谢组里每一位同事的热心照顾以及细心的教导，也祝池总及单位里的每个人万事如意，公司越办越

have gained is the friendship and mutual help. I haven't got the chance to compare you with other bosses, but your team is absolutely not unkind as imagined in traditional workplace. I remember my father's words that you are more like a "scholarly businessman" because of your educational background, and now through my personal experience I could certainly understand the unique team atmosphere and corporate spirit. What I remember most is the scene we went to have lunch together every day. The relaxing topics at the table, and the way we walked side by side in the shade of trees made one feel that it was more like a clear, pure high-school afternoon. The internship experiences I learned previously from senior students were more about the severe and stiff atmosphere, and I did not know any one company whose members would sit round one table and have lunch together in such a frank manner. In fact, this daily-life scene is far better than many "corporate teambuilding" in name only. Maybe my understating is still superficial, and I do not know whether I will be changed by society to become a short-sighted person who is always anxious to get quick results. But at least I will think of the quiet summer afternoon when I recall this period of experience many years later.

I have yet many unspoken words, which are finally turned into "Thank you." I am very grateful to the warm care and meticulous guidance given by

好，公司的经营范围扩展至世界的更多角落。谢谢能给我，一个不谙世事的准毕业生一个踏入社会的机会，以后的职场生活还在等着我去探寻，或好或坏，但是至少我走出去的第一步是一段美妙的开始。实迷途其未远，觉今是而昨非，为赋新词强说愁的现在的我也会带着这份期待和回忆继续向前……

希望每个人都顺顺利利，日后如果有需要我的地方我也非常乐意帮助，在上海见面的机会也有很多，都说分别是为了更好的相聚，下次聚首又是一年花开时！

every colleague in my team. I wish you and everyone at CNOOD good luck, and I wish CNOOD all the best of prosperity, reaching more corners all over the world. Thank you for giving me, who is still an inexperienced graduate, an opportunity to step into society. A career, good or bad, is waiting for me to explore; at least my first step marks the beginning of a marvelous journey. "Only a short distance have I gone astray, and I know today I am right, if yesterday was a complete mistake." Now, as a young person who would "pretend sadness to write a new song" would move forward with this expectation and remembrance.

I wish everyone all the best of success, and I will be more than willing to offer help in the future. We still have many chances to meet here in Shanghai. People say that separation is for a better reunion. When we meet again, it will be in the season of full bloom!

周 创
Zhou Chuang

周创，上海人，2018年毕业于英国伦敦大学学院统计专业，本科，CNOOD2018年暑期实习生

Born in Shanghai, Zhou Chuang graduated from University College London (UCL) majoring in Statistics, and was a summer intern at CNOOD in 2018.

春节小记
Spring Festival

■ Sissi Wu

回乡

南浦的艳阳天像个迎接新婚妻子的新郎，热情得可以瞬间把我融化。

我用蕴藏了一年的思念回应他。

青山秀，碧水蓝。

红灯笼，高高挂。

田野间，笑声扬。

你是否还记得最初的模样？

Back to My Old Home

The bright sunny skies at Nanpu, like a newly-married bridegroom who comes out to meet his wife, are so warm as to make me melt in a moment.

I respond to him with the longing that I have been keeping for one year.

The hills are green, the waters blue.

Red lanterns hang aloft.

Laughter could be heard among the fields.

Do you member the original appearance of my old home?

祭祖

元月初一，禅林深院。

父亲和我，登高祭祖。

大大的影子是父亲，小小的影子是我。

思绪爬进历史，重重叠叠好多影子，祖祖辈辈都在这片沃土扎根，越扎越深。

吴氏家族的历史印记敲在我们的心里，时光啊时光，我无从触摸你的面庞。

湖面上的水鸭一定被弄糊涂了

你看他那在水中呆呆的样子

相聚

花正艳，春意浓。

会老友，谢恩师。

一杯丹桂，四世同堂。

最爱街边烧烤摊，烟雾缭绕，那是属于故乡的云卷云舒。

锣鼓喧天的狂欢，我在听鞭炮声，鞭炮在追赶我的脚步。

Ancestor-Worshipping Ceremony

On the first day of the first month in Chinese lunar calendar, in the spacious courtyard of a Buddhist temple,

Father and I climb up to offer sacrifices to our ancestors.

The larger shadow is Father's, the smaller one is mine.

Our thoughts are crowded with history, with a myriad of overlapping shadows. All our ancestors, generation after generation, took roots in this fertile land, deeper and deeper.

The mark of the history of the Wu family has been stamped on our minds. O times, I cannot touch your face.

The teal on the surface of the lake must be confused,

Just look at it, who appears dumb-struck.

Get-Together

Flowers are in full bloom, while spring is very much in the air.

I meet my old friends, and express my gratitude to my old teacher.

With a cup of sweet osmanthus tea, four generations of a family gather under one roof.

I like most the barbecue booths along the streets veiled in smoke, which are the clouds belonging to my old home, now folding, now scattering.

Amid the deafening sound of gongs and drums, I am listening to the splutter of firecrackers; my footsteps are chased

离乡

春雨恰逢时节的酝酿，拂过耳旁。
像是催人离别的钟声，轻轻敲响。
我把我梦里的低语，留在小小的南浦县城。
这样
每次归途都能遥望，故乡最初的模样。
还可以
怀揣着梦的花苞，含苞待放。

Leaving My Old Home Again

The spring rain, brewed in the right season, is kissing my ears.

Its gentle sound, like that of chimes, urges people to part.

I have left my whispers in my dream at the little town of Nanpu.

Then

I can look from far away at its original appearance every time I go back to my old home.

And

I can have buds of dream in the bosom, ready to burst by them.

吴 茜 / Sissi Wu

慢热，但适应能力强；怀旧，但不喜欢一成不变。内心情感坚韧炙热，但从不轻易释放。偏像双子的金牛座，一半稳重，一半分裂。

Sissi is a person who warms up slowly but with a strong ability to adapt to different circumstances; while nostalgic for the past, she does not like invariability. Though filled with firm, passionate sentiments, she never releases them rashly. She is a Taurus closer to Gemini, half steady and half schizophrenic.

我的父亲
My Father

■ Dennis Chi

又见父亲，于梦里。大雪纷飞季，万家团圆时。

"绿蚁新醅酒，红泥小火炉。晚来天欲雪，能饮一杯无。"每待此刻，爸爸便让酿酒师傅准备"头子酒"，口感醇厚之极。一至家，爸爸延至上席，我偏坐陪席，聊过往今生，聊生活点滴。

5岁，学前，夏日，辰时，竹床在场院，乘凉。照例，又围在您身边。抑扬顿挫的声调，跌宕起伏的情节，薛丁山征西，秦琼卖马，罗士信力大无穷，李元霸

Once again, I met my Father; ---but in the dream. With big flakes of snow in the sky, it is now the season for family reunion.

"My new brew gives green glow;
My red clay stove flames up.
At dusk it threatens snow.
Won't you come for a cup?"

Every time when we celebrate the Spring Festival, Father would ask the distiller to prepare "head liquor", i.e. the first condensed liquor from distillation, which has a smooth, mellow flavor. As soon as I was back home, Father would take the seat of honor and I would sit beside him. We talked about the past and the present, and about tiny things in our lives.

When I was five-year-old pre-school boy, you and I would put a bamboo bed in the threshing ground and enjoy the cool in summer morning. I always sat beside

又力大无穷，罗成小心眼，誓语成谶，徐国公妙计安天下，一个个鲜活的人物，一个个灵动的故事，"仁义礼智信"，慢慢明白，智能定国，仁安天下，交友以义，立身处事，信义为先。

8岁，3年级，暑假，晌午，闲坐在宽敞的厅堂，任夏日的和风穿堂而过。"疾风知劲草，板荡识诚臣"，您忽而问我是何意。"大风，知道草的力量；磨炼，可以看出人的忠诚。"我脱口而出，带着自信，满脸不屑与傲气。"不错"，这是永远的标准评价，随着支楞的胡须节律地抖动，分明透着执着、坚毅。大风，自然知道草的力量。磨炼，会看出人的忠诚。而草呢，总会经历风霜雨雪，风霜雨雪，让草更加有生命力。没有雪的覆盖，麦田会歉收，会长虫，会倒伏。人，往高处走，活到老，学到老，不停上进；水，往低处流，心思放平，谦虚，才能进步；傲气，使人落后。人，不可以有傲气，但不能

you, enjoying the stories with fascinating plots, told in your well-modulated tone: How Xue Dingshan made his expedition to the west; how Qin Qiong sold his horse; how Luo Shixin showed his enormous strength; how Li Yuanba showed his enormous strength, too; how Luo Cheng, with petty calculations, was killed when young, turning his oath into a fulfilled augury; and how Xiao Yu stabilized the empire with his wisdom. Vivid figures in your lively account of history demonstrated the traditional noble characters of "benevolence, righteousness, propriety, wisdom and trustworthiness". I gradually understood that by wisdom can one settle the state affairs, by benevolence can one make the whole country tranquil, by righteousness should one make friends, and when dealing with things trustworthiness and righteousness are of first importance.

When I was eight years old and was a third-grade pupil, you and I would sit leisurely in the spacious hall at noon in summer days, with the gentle wind blowing through the hall. "What do you think," you suddenly asked me, "does the old saying 'As the force of the wind tests the strength of grass, so a man proves his loyalty in times of turbulence' mean?" "Only the strong wind knows the strength of the grass, and through trials and tribulations can a man's loyalty be revealed." I blurted the answer out confidently, with scorn and arrogance. "That's right" was your

没有傲骨。一个难得的中午，一直铭记于心，似懂非懂。在经历了许多的磨炼，许多的考试，回首那个中午，依然忘不了，那永远透着执着，蕴藏坚毅的支楞的胡须。那个中午，伴我走过许多春秋冬夏，陪我度过许多风霜雨雪，努力奋斗，永不放弃。

　　17岁，夏，收早稻。稻田淤泥，一脚上去，没过膝盖。斜着身子，用冲担挑起一端，奋力上肩，靠紧背脊，握紧冲担，俯下身，对准稻捆腰眼，深深扎下，抓住

invariable standard assessment. With your beard standing on end, shaking with rhythmic movement, I could tell the apparent perseverance and determination. The strong wind surely knows the strength of the grass, and through trials and tribulations can a man's loyalty be revealed. And the grass is bound to undergo adverse weather, which adds to the vitality of the grass. Without the covering of snow, we would have a bad harvest of wheat, as a result of insect pest and lodging. One should, as the saying goes, "hitch one's wagon to a star," and keep learning while one lives with continuous progress. On the other hand, one should remain calm and modest, just like water which always goes toward a lower place. Modesty helps one move forward whereas arrogance makes one lag behind. While one should not be arrogant, he must maintain a lofty and unyielding character. What happened in that afternoon has been stamped on my mind ever since, even if I did not fully understand what it meant at that time. I am still not able to forget Father's beard, standing on end and showing great perseverance and determination. That afternoon has afterwards been with me for many years and through a lot of hardships, encouraging me to work hard and never give up.

　　When I was seventeen years old, you and I would go out to reap the early rice in summer. We could feel the knee-deep silt in the paddy field as soon as we set

稻捆，起身，再担到岸上等候装车。水势较大，稻捆很湿，自然很重。看着您很轻松的样子，我依样画葫芦，没曾想洋相一箩筐。领略到劳动的艰辛，对生活的珍惜。

20岁，夏。第三次高考，再次以几分之差，名落孙山。呆呆地坐在厅堂里，努力地想着，错在哪里，想着是去做学徒，还是开餐馆。最终，您和妈妈，借了3 200元，让我上了大学。无以名状，无法想象，在那个年代里，如何筹集到这样一笔巨款；在那样的年代里，向谁筹集这样的巨款；在那样的年代里，到哪里筹集这样的巨款。这，展开了我人生的视野，意识到，知识的重要，努力的重要，坚持的重要；不管在如何困难的环境，不管在如何艰难的境遇，始终阔步前行，昂首挺胸，从不气馁，充满自信。

从没有听到，任何抱怨；从没看到，

foot in it. You bent sideways, picked up a bundle of rice straw with one end of chongdan (a kind of carrying pole with two pointed ends) and exerted yourself to lift it onto the shoulder. Then with the chongdan close to your backbone you bent over again and stabbed deep into another bundle of straw, before you stood up straight and carried the two bundles to the riverside to be loaded. The flow of water was strong, and the straw bundles became very heavy because of the moisture. I tried to copy what you did in a seemingly easy manner, only to make a fool of myself. From this episode did I taste the hardship of labor and know that we should cherish our life.

When I was twenty years old, I failed again in the university entrance examination in summer. Feeling completely at a loss, I sat in the hall and tried hard to figure out where I did wrong. I wondered what I should do next: to be an apprentice? or to open a restaurant? In the end, you and Mother managed to borrow 3,200 yuan to send me to college. It was hard to imagine how, from whom and where you two could raise such a big fund in those days. It broadened my horizon and made me fully aware of the importance of knowledge, effort, and persistence. Whatever adverse circumstances I might face, I should always stride proudly ahead with my chin up and chest out and should never lose heart.

I have never heard you complain or

任何埋怨。草，总会经历狂风骤雨；人，总有悲欢离合。即使在病重，神志不清的时候，也没有任何的埋怨。

您，只上过5年的私塾，学什么像什么，做什么精什么。泥匠，瓦匠，木匠，门门精；诗词，歌赋，戏曲，样样会。总想着，如何做到这些，如何能不骄不躁。

父爱如山，大爱如斯。我的岁月静好，是父亲的负重前行。

grumble about anything or anybody. Just as the grass is bound to experience violent storms, so people are bound to have joys and sorrows, partings and reunions. You never complained even in a trance when you were seriously ill.

As a person who only attended an old-style tutorial school for five years, you did a good job in everything you learned and was engaged. You were a fine plasterer, bricklayer, and carpenter; you were a master in traditional poems, songs and operas. I always wonder how you could achieve this without getting conceited at all.

The love of Father is like mountains, and great love is just like this. I could have my peaceful and good days only because Father was shouldering the burden for me.

池勇海
Dennis Chi

池勇海，男，汉族，1970年生于湖北省仙桃市。武汉理工大学管理学硕士，硕士导师刘国新教授；复旦大学经济学博士，博士导师洪远朋教授。2008年创立施璐德亚洲有限公司，现担任施璐德亚洲有限公司董事长。

Dennis Chi, of Han nationality, was born in Xiantao, Hubei Province in 1970. He received his Master's degree in Management Science at Wuhan University of Technology, where he studied under Professor Liu Guoxin, and received his PhD in Economics at Fudan University, where he studied under Professor Hong Yuanpeng. Dennis is now Chairman of CNOOD ASIA LIMITED, which he founded in 2008.

母亲节 让我为你写首诗

It's Mother's Day; Let Me Write You a Poem

■ Tony Liu

小时候
你爱我，是记忆中伴我入眠的故事和儿歌

上学时
你爱我，是十年一日寒暑不易的早餐与晚餐

大学时
你爱我，是回家后的唠叨和临别前的叮咛

工作后
你爱我，是微信里小心翼翼的问候"在忙吗？"

你爱我，
从花样青春
到韶华不再
从朝朝暮夕
到相悬两地

你把我带到这个缤纷的世界

When I was a baby
You loved me, with bedtime stories and nursery rhymes that still remain in my memory.

When I went to school
You loved me, with the breakfasts and suppers you prepared for me for ten years.

When I was a college student
You loved me, with the chatter when I'm at home and admonitions when you saw me off.

After I started my career
You have loved me, by cautiously asking me on WeChat: "Are you busy now?"

You love me
From the flower of life
To an age when the glorious youth has gone;
From our being together all day long
To staying in two different places.

You brought me to this colorful

我却为了梦想
慢慢地走向
你难以触及的远方

（才发现在梦里
常常又回到故乡
你的身旁）
这一次
你爱我
我想从右往左读

world,
And yet to pursue my dreams
I have been slowly moving
To a remote place which it is hard for you to reach.
(And then I realize that in dream
I often go back to the old home
To be with you.)
This time
The words "You love me"
Are to be read from the right end.

刘彬
Tony Liu

刘彬，别名观棋柯烂，好古文，寄情于松桂云壑。毕业于上海大学，2016年加入施璐德。

Tony, aka "A Woodcutter Watching the Chess Game Long Ago", is fond of Chinese ancient proses and finds enjoyment in natural scenery such as "pine trees, sweet-scented osmanthus, and valleys shrouded in clouds". He graduated from Shanghai University and joined CNOOD in 2016.

小诗四首
Four Poems

■ Tony Liu

贺中秋
——时惟八月，序属仲秋，花好月圆，共贺佳节。

皓月当空，明镜高悬
山河影曳，万里银川
玉宇琼楼，梦萦九天
冰鉴银盘，心思（施）故园

游子归乡，露（璐）从今夜白
天涯共此，月是故乡明
但得（德）人长久
千里共婵娟

观棋柯烂
——独在异乡为异客，每逢佳节倍思亲。已经在外十年了，七年求学，三年从业，辗转于天南地北。时光荏苒，寒暑相易，记忆中的中秋节还停留在儿时在外婆家一家团聚的模样，从前月饼，桂酒的味道早已淡忘，唯有对外婆的思念一直悬挂

Celebrating the Moon Festival

—It is the eighth month of the year, or the Mid-Autumn, when flowers are blooming and the moon is full. Let's celebrate the happy festival together.

The bright moon, like a clear mirror, hangs in the sky;

Mountains and rivers throw their shadows across the vast silvery plains.

I dream of the crystalline palace high above in the heaven;

Looking at the icy moon, I miss my old home.

Dew turns into frost since tonight;

Watch the moon far and near, east and west, you and I. The moon viewed at home is brighter.

So let's wish that man live as long as he can!

Though miles apart, we'll share the beauty she displays.

A Woodcutter Who Watched a Go Game Long Ago

—"Alone, a lonely stranger in a foreign land, I doubly pine for kinsfolk on a holiday." I have been away from my old home for ten years, seven years for my studies, three years at work, during which

在心间。

time I moved from place to place across the country. Time flies, but the Moon Festival in my memory is still about the scenes of family reunion at my grandma's in my childhood. The flavor of the mooncakes and osmanthus-flower wine have long been forgotten; however, I have been missing my grandma ever since.

小溪的水

逆流而上
纷飞的桂花
飘回枝桠
聚成盛开的模样
蒸汽飘回机舱
渡轮回到母港
我交回录取通知书
忘了十年寒窗
你静坐在溪旁
浆洗沾满泥土的衣裳
我光着背膀
在树下乘凉
厨房飘来陶罐饭的焦香
你还在我身旁

The water in the creek
Goes upstream.
The swirling osmanthus flowers
flutter back to their branches
and cluster together as in full bloom.
The steam floats back to the engine room
as the ferryboat is returning to its home port.
I give back my admission notice sent by the college
forgetting the hardships when I persevered in my studies.
Quietly you sit by the creek
washing the clothes covered in mud stains.
Naked to the waist, I
enjoy the cool in the shade of a big tree.
A pleasant smell of burnt pot-rice wafts from the kitchen.
You are still there with me.

庆华诞

十里长街沐芬芳
九重天阙吐霞光
八河舸舰弥津上
七千州县谱华章

Happy Birthday
The Chang'an Avenue, ten miles long, is bathed in fragrance;
Ancient palaces reflect the shining rays of morning sunlight.

六路五关龙虎骧
四海三江锦鳞翔
两岸同胞共遥望
一面红旗迎风扬

Ships and boats from all rivers come together at the port;

A gorgeous cadenza is composed by the people across our country.

Dragons and tigers gallop along many roads and passes;

Colorful fish glide in the Four Seas and Three Rivers.

Compatriots from both sides of the Strait look afar together;

A red flag fluttering in the breeze.

初心·2019 元旦序

月正元日
光华旦始
数不尽春光 门前绿树阶前玉树
看将来气象 千里晴云万里青云
十年一剑 不忘初心
千里之路 止于至善

Original Aspiration: A prologue to the New Year of 2019

On the first day of the first moon in the year,

Everything is having a fresh beginning in splendor.

Spring is in the air, with green and jade-like trees in front of doors;

Looking forward, we see thousands and tens of thousands of clear sky with white clouds

Spending ten years to make a sword, we stay true to our original aspiration;

Setting out on a journey of ten thousand miles, we will not stop until we achieve the supreme excellence.

刘 彬
Tony Liu

刘彬，别名观棋柯烂，好古文，寄情于松桂云壑。毕业于上海大学，2016年加入施璐德。

Tony, aka "A Woodcutter Watching the Chess Game Long Ago", is fond of Chinese ancient proses and finds enjoyment in natural scenery such as "pine trees, sweet-scented osmanthus, and valleys shrouded in clouds". He graduated from Shanghai University and joined CNOOD in 2016.

亚沙随笔

Random Writings About Asian-Pacific Business Schools Desert Challenge

■ Tony Liu

2018年五一劳动节期间（4.29～5.1），秉承公司一贯践行的"相互关心，创造开心"的理念，CNOOD赞助并联合上海对外经贸大学MBA学员参加了第7届亚太地区商学院沙漠挑战赛"（简称"沙7"）。亚沙赛是在亚太地区商学院的MBA学员群体中展开的一项竞技体验式文化赛事。同各校参赛的MBA学员通过徒步穿越70余公里沙漠的竞技比赛，亲自体验和践行"环保、协作、坚持、责任"的赛事理念。

Adhering to its philosophy of "Caring Number of Others' Delightfulness, Creating New Ocean of Delightfulness", CNOOD sponsored the Seventh Asian-Pacific Business Schools Desert Challenge and participated in it along with MBA candidates from Shanghai University of International Business and Economics (SUIBE) during the May Day vacation (April 29 to May 1) in 2018. The Challenge is a cultural sport event for MBA candidates of business schools in the Asian-Pacific region. Participants are required to cover a distance of over 70 kilometers on foot, personally experience and implement the event's idea of "environmentally friendliness, cooperation, perseverance, and responsibility."

一 初见银川

我只在书本和诗文里见过塞北。

这是我第一次来塞北,跟随着"牛排"参加沙7。从上海到银川,下了飞机后就上了大巴直奔阿拉善盟。道路两旁的白桦树摇曳生姿,小河绿草环绕,波光粼粼,闻名不如见面,果然一幅塞上江南的气息,暂未逢大漠孤烟,长河落日,直到大巴驶至贺兰山麓,环顾四下,我才感受到诗里的那座银川:

1. A First Glance at Yinchuan

I have seen the land north of the Great Wall only in books and verses.

This is my first time to visit a place north of the Great Wall, taking part in the Seventh Asian-Pacific Business Schools Desert Challenge as a member of "Rampage." We get on the bus heading for Alxa League ("league" is a prefecture-level administrative division in the Inner Mongolia Autonomous Region), as soon as we go off the plane after flying from Shanghai to Yinchuan. White birches along both sides of the road sway in the wind, and the creeks, with limpid ripples, are embellished with green grass along both sides. The "Southern Scenery Beyond the Great Wall" is indeed more attractive than I have imagined. We have not yet seen "a smoke hanging straight on the vast desert" and "a sun sitting round on the endless stream." It is at the foot of

俯凭驼铃临河套

遥带银川挹贺兰

函谷玉门堪鼎足

金城百二入安澜

二 过贺兰山

大巴在贺兰山中蜿蜒前行，望着窗外跌宕起伏的群山，晴云万里的天空，我整个心里惟有剩下那一首《老将行》：

贺兰山下阵如云

羽檄交驰日夕闻

节使三河募年少

诏书五道出将军

那一刻，我仿佛身处于古战场，看风起云涌，听铁马金戈，如南柯一梦。

the Helanshan Mountain that I, looking around, begin to know about Yinchuan, a city depicted in the verse:

> Amidst caravan bells we approach the Great Bend of the Yellow River,
> Beyond the Silver Plain a distant belt girdles the Helanshan Mountain.
> The Changcheng Pass, together with the renowned Hangu and Yumen
> Forms an impregnable fortress, bringing peace to people of Cathay.

2. Across the Helanshan Mountain

The bus is zigzagging among the ranges of Helanshan Mountain. What is left solely in my mind is a verse from "The Old General" by Wangwei, while I am gazing at the rolling mountains and the blue, cloudless skies outside the window:

> Below Helanshan, like gathering clouds, Units were deployed in battle array.
> Urgent orders flashed across the whole land.
> Such things we were given to know, night and day.
> Ministers at Henei, Henan, Hedong—
> Were to carry out vast recruiting plans.
> An edict commissioned five generals—
> To take command against the foe's advance.

At this moment, I feel as if I were at an ancient battlefield, looking at the rising wind and surging clouds and listening to the noise of battle, just like in a fast vanishing dream.

三 阿拉善盟

越过贺兰山，我们就进入内蒙古境内了，不多久就到了阿拉善左旗，映入眼帘的一个巨大的天马行空铜雕，写着天山圣地，一片繁荣昌盛之景，我还以为戈壁千里、黄沙漫漫呢？看来今夜要借宝地落脚了。

3. The Alxa League

Going across the Helanshan Mountain we are now in the Inner Mongolia Autonomous Region. When we arrive in Alxa Left Banner ("banner" is a county-level administrative division in the Inner Mongolia Autonomous Region), what meets the eye is a huge bronze statue of a heavenly steed soaring across the skies, with four characters meaning "A Sacred Place at the Tianshan Mountain." Instead of being a little town among the vast Gobi with thousands of miles of yellow sand, it is really a bustling city. It seems that we have to find a hotel here to

夜暮降临，华灯初上，阿拉善更是美的有点不像话，一点儿也不输那古都大邑：

春城无处不飞花

寒食东风御柳斜

日暮汉宫传蜡烛

轻烟散入五侯家

四　相逢腾格里

其实在进入沙漠之前我对待亚沙的态度一直很随意，在我眼中，亚沙不过是观光旅行，聊天拍照，用以赚点噱头的资本而已，所以我没有做运动准备，也没有在意装备，更没有斗志昂扬。我就是在这种状态进入沙漠的，直到我跪在了第一个关卡，我才真正认真地对待它，后面的四关对我来说，用步履维艰来形容一点也不过分，直到关门前一刻钟我才到达终点，瘫倒在营地的我久久站不起来，望着长空中孤悬的月影，我才意识到这并不是场游戏，而是场运动竞技，挑战的便是在这屹立了千年的腾格里沙漠，今夜并不是结束，而是刚刚开始。

stay the night.

When the night falls, Alxa, decorated with colorful evening lights, is beautiful beyond description, not the least inferior to those ancient capitals or big cities:

There's nowhere in spring town but flowers fall from trees;
On Cold Food Day royal willows slant in east breeze.
At dusk the palace sends privileged candles red
To the five lordly mansions where wreaths of smoke spread.

4. A Rendezvous at the Tengger

In fact, I took a rather casual attitude toward the Challenge before I come into the desert. To me the Challenge is no more than a sight-seeing and photo-taking tour with little chit-chats, which I can boast for. As a result, I did not do any physical training, nor did I pay much attention to the sport equipment, not to say the lack of high fighting spirit. I have entered the desert in such a frame of mind and have not taken it seriously until I collapse at the first checkpoint. It would be no overstatement if I say I have passed the following four checkpoints "with every step made with difficulty." I come to the finish line only 15 minutes before the close time. I feel weak in the knees and lie on the ground of the camping site for a long time, unable to get up. Staring at the lonely moon in the sky, I realize that it is not a mere game; it is a true sport, and we are launching a challenge

toward the thousands-year-old Tengger Desert. Tonight is not the end; it is just the beginning.

五　雄关漫道

黑云压城城欲摧
甲光向日金鳞开
报君黄金台上意
提携玉龙为君死

5. An Iron-clad Pass

*Black clouds loom heavy over the city,
And the city on the verge of caving in,
Armors gleam golden with open scales in the sun.
To return the favor on the Golden Stage,
I tote my Jade-Dragon sword to die for him.*

第二天，早上 8：00，沙漠气温 15°，风速 6.5 m/s，阴沉的云层遮掩着太阳，将出未出。勇士们虽然略显疲惫，但仍然整装待发，我也紧随其后，越过沙丘，河流，盐地。从寒意萧然的清晨到烈日当头的正午，再到下午，直到终点。当翻过最后一座高高的沙丘，我在沙丘上伫立着，前面就是旌旗飘扬的营地，示意着今天 28 公里的终结，疲惫的身心瞬时备受鼓舞，回顾身后，是一望无垠的大漠和湛蓝远空，云淡风轻，心旷神怡。

At 8 o'clock in the morning of next day, the temperature in the desert is 15 degrees Celsius and the wind speed is 6.5 meters per second. The sun is hiding behind the gloomy clouds, hesitant to come out. The brave men and women, though a little fatigued, are all ready to set out. I closely follow them and trudge across sand dunes, creeks and saline field. After a long day from the chilly morning to the scorching noon, and later to the afternoon, I finally reach the finish line. After climbing over the last high sand dune, I stand alone on its top. Right in front of me is the camping site with flying flags and banners, indicating the conclusion of the 28-kilometer course today. All of a sudden, I feel greatly encouraged while extremely tired. Looking back, I can see a vast expanse of desert and blue sky stretching as far as the horizon. With the pale clouds and gentle breeze, I am refreshed in mind and heart.

由于第三天只有10公里,基本上如探囊取物了,所以今晚便可以开始狂欢了,夜慢慢地来了,一年一度的沙漠晚会便在众人的期待中开始了。晚会的内容是来自各个高校的沙友精心准备的各种节目,载歌载舞,霓虹闪烁,放眼望去,营地的帐篷被映成了五光十色,尽头是连绵起伏的沙丘,沙丘接连着一片片云层,托出一轮明月,静静地遥望着我们这群不知疲倦的人儿。

It will be quite easy day for the third day since we need cover only 10 kilometers. Therefore, we begin our carnival tonight. Slowly the darkness of night settles over the land, and the once-in-a-year desert gala opens as we expected. During the gala participants from different universities give a brilliant performance with all kinds of well-prepared programs. With songs and dances amid the neon lights, I see the tents in the camping site become multi-colored, and there are, as far as the eye

could see, rolling sand dunes, melting into clouds, with a bright moon hanging against the infinite darkness of the sky, which looks down quietly at us, a group of tireless people.

六 告别

预料之中，第三天的赛程很快就结束了。在终点，我再一次看到那久违的笑容又重新浮现在那一张张可爱的面庞上，充满着感动和喜悦，像是身心都在沙漠中涅槃新生一般。我是打心里为他们感到高兴，可是不知道为什么当披上奖牌时，我的心情却十分平静，我甚至能听到自己的

6. Bidding Farewell

The third day quickly comes to an end as expected. At the finish line, I see again the smiles, which I haven't seen for a couple of days, on the lovely faces. I am filled with excitement and joy, as if my body and soul have been reborn in the desert. I feel happy for them; but for

心跳。亚沙结束了，我要和腾格里说再见了，心里反倒有些不舍了，也许对我来说结局并没有那么重要，最享受的是那挥洒汗水的竞技过程、沿途的风景和那些陪伴我身边的朋友和家人。

unknown reasons, I am extremely calm when I am presented a medal. I am so calm that I can even hear my heart beat. The Challenge is over; now I shall say goodbye to the Tengger Desert. However, I feel a little reluctant to leave. Maybe to me the result is not that important; what really matters is the process of sweating, the beautiful scenery, and my friends and family who have been with me during these days.

后记

这三天我跟随了很多勇士

Postscript

I have followed many brave men and women from

湖大，南大，重大，北航…

那些时刻
我仿佛变成了一个木偶
心里没有任何东西
没有工作，没有篮球，也没有她
只有下一个脚印
直到他们选择停了下来
我只能做自己的勇士

亚沙，改日再战！

Hunan University, Nanjing University, Chongqing University, Beihang University...

I feel as if I became a puppet at that time
With my mind devoid of anything:
Work, basketball, and her,
Except for a next footstep.
I could be only my own brave man
Before they choose to have a stop.

I shall return.

刘彬
Tony Liu

刘彬，别名观棋柯烂，好古文，寄情于松桂云壑。毕业于上海大学，2016年加入施璐德。

Tony, aka "A Woodcutter Watching the Chess Game Long Ago", . is fond of Chinese ancient proses and finds enjoyment in natural scenery such as "pine trees, sweet-scented osmanthus, and valleys shrouded in clouds". He graduated from Shanghai University and joined CNOOD in 2016.

永远停不下的脚步
Footsteps That Would Never Stop

■ Billy Gu

亚沙的感悟:

从来就不是你一个人在跑，
从来也不是和谁在比拼，

从来也不是为了证明什么，

在你决定坚持的那一刹那，

已经没有理由让自己停下脚步。

What I understand about the Asian-Pacific Business Schools Desert Challenge:

You are never alone in running,

You are never competing with anybody else,

It's never for the purpose of proving something,

There has been no reason to stop your footsteps

Since the moment you decided to hold on.

之前参加过第六届亚沙，曾给我很多启发，经历过坎坷与绝望，并在希望和忍耐中完成了比赛。带着必胜的决心来参加第七届亚沙，开始并没有很复杂的焦虑。却在第一天的比赛中就已经超过了比赛规定的时间达半小时。就像在警醒我，永远别太自信而变得自大。

不服输的我，并不想要退缩，脑子里只想走完比赛，哪怕就只能多走一步。当最后一天在规定比赛时间内走完时，也感觉值了。

最难忘的画面：第一天最后一个CP的路上，见到了许多沙友坐在地上在等待收容车，也许那时已经知道无法在有效时间内走到终点了，也许沙鸥和我们并没有关系了，也许个人的成绩将被清零，但总有那么一个声音在耳边回荡，走下去，坚持下去。于是我对每一位沙友们都说："加油走下去，快到了。"感觉我鼓励着他们但这正是在鼓励自己，当最后很多沙友重新站起来决定继续走下去的时候，那是我最幸福的时刻。能将正能量传递给别人的幸福感。

I took part in the sixth Asian-Pacific Business Schools Desert Challenge, which proved to be a most inspirational experience for me. With hope and endurance, I finished the challenge after going through setbacks and despair. I came to the seventh Challenge with a resolute mind to win, and did not have any anxiety. However, in the first day, I spent half an hour more than the maximum time allowed. It was a warning: never be over-confident and become conceited.

As a person who never accepts failure, I did not want to shrink back; all I was thinking about was to finish the challenge even if I could only walk one single step further. When I finished the course within the maximum time allowed, I felt that it was worth the effort.

The most unforgettable scene: On the first day, I saw many runners sitting on the ground waiting for the sweeper bus along the way toward the last check point. Maybe at that time we knew we would never be able to reach the finish line within the effective time limit, maybe the seagull had nothing to do with us, or maybe our personal result will be zero, but there was still a voice ringing around my ear: "Keep on walking, and hold on." I then said to everyone: "Come on! Keep walking! We are near the finish line." It seemed that I was encouraging them; in fact, I was encouraging myself at the same time. When eventually many fellow participants stood up again and decided

亚沙是个能给自己感悟的机会的平台，亚沙让我更安静地观察自己，更深刻地认知自己，更全面地反思自己。

参加亚沙后更坚持了自己在锻炼上的决心。

to go on, it was my happiest moment. It was a happiness of delivering positive energy to others.

The Challenge is a platform which gives me the chance to perceive and understand certain things. It makes me observe myself more quietly, know myself more deeply, and reflect on myself more thoroughly.

I have become more determined to continue physical exercises ever since.

顾天阳
Billy Gu

2010年正式加入CNOOD工作至今，现为高级客户经理，学历MBA。见证了CNOOD每一次起点，每一次奇迹的发生。从一般贸易到工程贸易，从工程贸易到项目采购中心，现在又在为公司成为真正的EPC工程公司而努力。相信：一切不是最好就没到最后。

Billy has been working at CNOOD ASIA LIMITED since he formally joined the company in 2010. Now he is a senior account manager in CNOOD with an MBA degree. He has witnessed everystarting pointof CNOOD and every time a miracle occurred.Having seen the transformation of CNOOD as a company focused on general trade to one engaged in engineering trade, and again to a project procurement center, now he is making efforts to help CNOOD become a true EPC company. He believes that it is not the end if everything is not the best.

CNOOD 代表团拜访罗马尼亚
——布加勒斯特市政府

CNOOD Delegates Visited Romania —At the City Hall of Bucharest

■ CNOOD News

罗马尼亚作为欧盟成员国，是中国同中东欧国家、乃至同整个欧洲合作的重要支点，也是"一带一路"倡议的重要沿线国家。

2015年，罗马尼亚经济部与中国商务部签署了关于在两国经济联委会下推进共建丝绸之路经济带的谅解备忘录，罗马尼亚成为首批与中国签署此类协议的国家。

2018年4月16日至20日，CNOOD合伙人刘威、CNOOD投融资部经理Danni Xu与中铁二十局、中国电力工程有限公司、中国建筑工程总公司的代表一起

As a member of the European Union (EU) and an important participating country in the Belt and Road Initiative, Romania plays a pivotal role in the cooperation between China and CEE countries and even the general Sino-European cooperation.

A memorandum of understanding for advancing the cooperation in Silk Road Economic Belt within the framework of China-Romanian Joint Economic Committee was signed between the Ministry of Economy of Romania and the Ministry of Commerce of People's Republic of China in 2015. Romania was the first country who signed similar agreement with China.

Max Liu, a partner of CNOOD, Danni Xu, Manager of the Department of Investment and Finance, together with representatives from China

罗马尼亚商会留影
左三为 CNOOD 合伙人刘威 Max Liu
Max Liu, a partner of CNOOD ASIA LIMITED (3rd from the left) at the Chamber of Commerce and Industry of Romania

拜访罗马尼亚首都布加勒斯特市政府以及当地工程、运输、能源公司。

布加勒斯特市市长对中国企业代表团表示诚挚的欢迎，并简要介绍了罗马尼亚大型工程项目，包括路桥建设、机场建设、高速公路建设、水利水电和新能源领域的国家投资项目。

Railway 20 Bureau Group Corporation, China National Electric Engineering Corporation and China State Construction Engineering Corporation, visited the City Hall of Bucharest and local engineering, logistics and energy companies during April 16-20, 2018.

The Mayor of Bucharest gave a heartfelt welcome to the delegation of Chinese enterprises and made a brief description of large-scale engineering projects in Romania, including state investment projects in various fields such as road and bridge construction, airport construction, expressway construction, water conservancy, hydropower generation and new energies.

目前罗马尼亚拥有很多工程项目机会。CNOOD可以抓住罗马尼亚基础设施建设的机遇，开拓罗马尼亚市场，并借助其地理位置优势，规划进入中东欧市场的长远战略。

At present there are many opportunities of engineering projects in Romania. CNOOD should try to grasp the opportunities in Romania's infrastructure construction and expand the market, while making long-term plans to enter CEE markets based on the geographic advantage of Romania.

Max 与 Dan Tudorache 市长交换名片
Max exchanging business cards with Mr. Dan Tudorache, Mayor of Bucharest

布加勒斯特市政厅
At the City Hall of Bucharest

举行座谈会
Holding the Conference

Grampet Group 留影
At Grampet Group

CNOOD 与上海财经大学经济学院签署战略合作协议

CNOOD Signed Strategic Cooperation Agreement with School of Economics, SUFE

■ CNOOD News

2018年6月22日上午，上海财经大学经济学院、高等研究院田国强院长，王昉书记，陈波教授以及王越男老师到访施璐德亚洲有限公司。双方本着发挥各自优势，加强产学研合作创新，共同推动上海财经大学经济学院、高等研究院教育科研事业的发展，并为施璐德亚洲有限公司提供相关领域人才培养服务及智力支持的宗旨，经过充分沟通、交流，决定建立合作伙伴关系，并签署了合作协议。

Professor Tian Guoqiang, Dean of the School of Economics (SOE) and the Institute for Advanced Research (IAR), Shanghai University of Finance and Economics (SUFE), Professor Wang Fang, CPC Committee Secretary of SOE, Professor Chen Bo, and Wang Yuenan, Administrative Director of IAR, visited CNOOD ASIA LIMITED on the morning of June 22, 2018. In order to give full play to their respective advantages, enhance innovation in industry-university-research collaboration, give further impetus to education and scientific research for SOE and IAR, and provide personnel training service and intelligent support for CNOOD ASIA LIMITED, the two parties decided, after in-depth communication, to build up a cooperative partnership and

双方的合作方式及内容包括但不限于建设高水平的师资队伍和决策咨询研究团队，联合培养人才，扩大社会影响、提升学术声誉，以及加强各自工会组织、校友组织等群团组织的交流与合作。

上海财经大学经济学院简介

上海财经大学的经济学教学与研究历史源远流长。早在上世纪 30 年代由著名经济学家马寅初担任国立上海商学院教务长时，就设立了经济研究室。1950 年 8 月，上海法学院财经系科并入，学院增设经济系。1951 年 6 月，经济系更名为经济计划系。1958 年 8 月，经济计划系随学校与华东政法学院合并成立上海社会科学院。1960 年重建上海财经学院，设商业经济等专业；1962 年夏，撤商业经济专业，设工业经济、贸易经济等专业，直到 1972 年 4 月随学校被撤销。1978 年复校，1980 年 2 月成立经济学系，由原经济学系、数量经济研究所合并组成。2000 年 4 月成立经济学院。

signed a strategic cooperation agreement.

The cooperation includes but is not limited to building a high-standard faculty and highly efficient decision-making advisory teams, nurturing talents in a joint manner, promoting their overall influence and academic reputation, and enhancing the communication and cooperation between their trade unions and alumni organizations.

About the School of Economics, Shanghai University of Finance and Economics (SUFE)

Shanghai University of Finance and Economics (SUFE) has a long history of teaching and research in economics. In the early thirties of the 20th century, when it was called National Shanghai College of Commence (NSCC), with the famous economist Ma Yinchu as its Dean of Studies, the Center for Economics Research was established. In August 1950, the finance and economics faculties of Shanghai College of Law were incorporated into NSCC, and the Faculty of Economics was established, which was renamed the Faculty of Economic Planning in June 1951. NSCC, with the Faculty of Economic Planning, merged with East-China College of Political Science and Law to form Shanghai Academy of Social Sciences in August 1958. Shanghai College of Finance and Economics (SCFE) was established in 1960, with disciplines including Commerce Economics, which was replaced by Industrial Economics

新中国成立后上海财政经济学院首任院长孙冶方，老一辈经济学家姚耐、孙怀仁、王惟中、杨荫溥、胡寄窗，经济学系首任系主任张淑智，经济学院历任院长程恩富、胡景北等为经济学院的发展奠定了坚实的基础。现任院长为"千人计划"国家特聘专家、长江学者讲座教授、美国得州A&M大学Alfred F. Chalk讲席教授田国强。

近年来，经济学院秉持"中国特色、世界一流、国家急需、服务社会"的发展方略，以"经济学创新平台"建设项目为载体，围绕"聚一流教师、汇一流学生、设一流课程、育一流人才、做一流研究、臻一流治理、创一流学科、建一流学院"的八个一流方针，全面开启了具有历史意义的体制内经济学教育科研改革，其宗旨就在于立足中国国情和学校实际，参照国际一流研究型大学先进的办学理念和成熟

and Trade Economics in the summer of 1962. SCFE was dissolved in April 1972 and reestablished in 1978. The Faculty of Economics and the Institute for Quantitative Economics were merged into the Department of Economics in February 1980, which was renamed the School of Economics (SOE) in April 2000.

Sun Yefang, the first Dean of Shanghai College of Finance and Economics (SCFE) after the founding of the People's Republic of China, renowned economists including Yao Nai, Sun Huairen, Wang Weizhong, Yang Yinpu and Hu Jichuang, as well as Zhang Shuzhi, the first Dean of the Faculty of Economics, and the former deans of SOE including Cheng Enfu, Hu Jingbei etc. have laid a solid for the development of SOE. Professor Tian Guoqiang has been the Dean of SOE since 2004. He is a distinguished professor of Thousand Talents Program and chair professor of Humanities and Social Sciences Changjiang Scholars, and Alfred F. Chalk professor of Economics of Department of Economics in A & M University.

In recent years, adhering to the development plan of "Chinese Characteristics, World Class, National Needs, and Social Service", and with the implementation of the special project "Economics Innovation Platform", SOE now endeavors under the guideline of "Eight First-Class", i.e. "recruiting first-class faculty and first-class students, offering first-class

的管理规范，实践教育科研改革，系统地建立一整套长效机制，致力于培养厚德博学的具有深厚文化素养、扎实经济学理论功底、高效生产力、开放国际视野的高素质创新型人才，打造国内顶尖、世界一流的有影响力的经济学院。

学院现有全职教研人员93人，其中特聘教授16人，中组部"千人计划"特聘专家5人，国务院特殊津贴专家4人，长江学者特聘教授2人，长江讲席教授4人，国家百千万人才工程1人，教育部新世纪优秀人才4人，上海市曙光学者2人。全职教师中，教授24人，副教授50人，教师中拥有海外博士学位的有60人，占比约64%。现有在册学生1 089名，本科生717名，研究生（含硕士生、硕博连读生、博士生）372名。

curriculum, nurturing first-class talents, doing first-class researches, achieving first-class governance, creating first-class disciplines, and becoming a first-class school of economics". Having initiated a historic reform of the teaching and research system, it aims, based on Chinese characteristics and the reality of SOE, to learn the advanced ideas and mature management norms of world's top universities, to carry out the reform of teaching and research system, to introduce systematic long-term mechanism, and finally, while being dedicated to the training of high-quality innovative talents, who strives for virtue and knowledge, with solid cultural attainments, a good grounding in economic theories, high productiveness, and open international vision, to become a top-notch school of economics both in China and in the world.

SOE is now the intellectual home of 93 faculty members, among whom there are 16 distinguished professors, five distinguished experts of Thousand Talents Program (by the Organization Department of CPC Central Committee), four State-Council Special Allowance Experts, two distinguished professors of Changjiang Scholars, four chair professors of Changjiang Scholars, one candidate for Millions of Talents Project, four professors supported by the Program for New Century Excellent Talents in University, and two Shanghai Twilight Scholars. In total there are 24 professors,

50 associate professors, while 60 of them hold PhDs from North American and European Universities, accounting for about 64% of the whole faculty. SOE now has 717 undergraduate students and 372 graduate students.

不忘初心
——记施璐德 2018 年新同事入职仪式
2018 年 8 月 8 日

Stay True to Our Original Aspiration:
The Welcome Ceremony for New Colleagues 2018
August 8, 2018

■ CNOOD News

10 年前的 8 月 8 日
是北京奥运会开幕的日子

2018 年的 8 月 8 日
在施璐德上海办公室
一家人欢聚一堂
为新同事举办入职欢迎仪式

新同事个人展示

August 8, 2008
Was the day when the Beijing Olympic Games was declared open.

August 8, 2018
Is the day when members of the CNOOD family get together joyously
For welcoming new colleagues.

Personal Presentation by Our New Colleagues

李堤　Dacre
上海大学环境工程硕士
Shanghai University
Master in Environmental Engineering

说起这个英文名字，大家一开始可能不敢去读、怕读错，大家可以叫我达克。

我来自上海大学，主修环境工程专业，硕士期间的研究方向是新能源。我平日的爱好是学习语言如日语，运动如格斗和跑步。

来公司实习也已有半年多了，对于个人的短期目标是做到三点：专注、专业及耐心。专注于某一领域，提升此领域的专业度，在不断提升专业度的过程中，耐心坚持下去。为了成长为一个公司人才，我觉得在之后的职业生涯中，我要改正自己粗心的缺点，做到细心负责，为人幽默，能综合各个领域的知识并高效地完成工作。

As for my English name, it's likely that you are afraid of pronouncing it in a wrong way. Relax and just call me "Dark".

I'm from Shanghai University majoring in Environmental Engineering. I studied new energy as a postgraduate student. My hobbies include learning foreign languages (e.g. Japanese) and sports (e.g. fighting and running).

It has been more than half a year since I began my internship at CNOOD, and my short-term goal is to become a person with devotion, expertise and patience, i.e. to devote myself to a specific area, promote expertise in it, and hold on with patience. In order to become a talent for the company, I must improve regarding my weak point of carelessness, and to be meticulous, responsible and humorous, able to integrate knowledge of various fields and work efficiently.

刘婷　Sophie
上海大学冶金工程硕士
Shanghai University
Master in Metallurgical Engineering

通过Tony知道了CNOOD的存在，因为宣讲会而进一步了解、认识了CNOOD，在宣讲会上与Allen和Billy的交流，让我当时产生一个疑问，真的有这样一个公司吗？而接下来，事实回答了我，真

I knew of CNOOD through Tony before I had a better understanding of it through campus recruitment road show. Talking with Allen and Billy made me doubt the existence of such a company.

的有。在年会的筹办过程以及年鉴的品读中，我又进一步感知CNOOD。在年鉴中，我看到了每一个人眼中的CNOOD，也因此更加深刻的感知了CNOOD的企业文化。就这样幸运的我与一个幸运的公司结缘了。

毕业以后，进入工作，面临从学生身份到一个职场人的转变。刚进公司，和同事们相处一段时间，就理解了公司的耀人业绩从何而来，是每一个同事严谨、认真的处事态度创造的。Carol耐心地跟我讲解执行中的项目概况，其他同事也很耐心的解答每一个甚至很细微的问题，这就让我可以更快的完成这样的转变，并且融入进来，在这个过程中，也在不断认识自己的不足，也在积极的学习。在公司给我们这样一个轻松自由平等的工作氛围中，也认识到更应该加强自我学习，找准自我定位。我们应该以一个新人的态度去持续的学习，而不是以一个新人的姿态去工作。

Later, facts told me that there was indeed such a company. Through the preparation of the annual meeting and the reading of *the CNOOD Yearbook*, I obtained a further understanding of CNOOD. In the *Yearbook*, I saw the CNOOD in the eyes of everybody, and thus had an even deeper perception of its corporate culture. This is how I—a lucky person—was connected with CNOOD—a lucky company.

I had to face the metamorphosis from a student to a professional after graduation. I understood the source of the brilliant performance of the company soon after I entered the company and worked with my colleagues for a short period of time. It was made possible by the meticulous, rigorous way of doing things of every colleague. Carol patiently explained to me the background of the on-going projects, and other people too patiently answered every detailed question for me, helping me go through the metamorphosis more quickly and mix in. In this process, I also noticed my shortcomings and learned in a positive manner. In such a relaxing, free, and democratic working atmosphere provided by the company, I know I should learn more and find my precise position. I should learn continuously as a newcomer but shall not work as a newcomer.

宋瑞文　Raven
中国石油大学（北京）油气田开发硕士
China University of Petroleum-Beijing
Master in Oil & Gas Development

七年石油专业的学习，在外人看来必将进入石油系统。有的朋友和家人会说我这七年"白学了"。然而我却不这么认为，学术的锻炼是塑造了一种思维一种能力，这才是我最终拥有的，而不是那些书本上的专业知识。

遇到施璐德之后，发生了很多难忘的第一次。2018年会上的First Show；人生第一次出差，独自去缅甸和业主面对面展示；以及在施璐德的第一份工作。人们都说，人生的第一家公司很重要，那经过这几个月，我觉得我的选择是正确的。

After seven years of studies in oil & gas development, I was expected to go into the oil & gas industry. As for my choice, some friends and family members would say that I had "studied in vain" during these years. However, I don't think so. The academic training has shaped a way of thinking and an ability for me; rather than the knowledge in the books, those are what I really have in the end.

There were many unforgettable "first's" after I encountered CNOOD: The first show in the 2018 annual meeting; the first business trip during which I flied to Myanmar by myself and gave face-to-face presentation to the project owner; and my first job at CNOOD. People say that the first company you work for in your life is very important. Now, after several months, I think I have made the right decision.

这张照片拍摄于缅甸出差归来的飞机上，朝阳就像我们的未来，耀眼、充满各种可能。

未来自己想成为：自律，有执行力，有逻辑的人。因为，自律才有自由，执行力才有结果，有逻辑才有体系。大部分人都渴望有一份稳定的工作，但是何为稳定的工作？我认为，稳定不是指稳定的收入，稳定的工作状态。而是拥有所长，拥有自身的核心竞争力和核心内核，并能够充分发挥自己的价值在未来的职业生涯中，这才是稳定。

This is a photo taken on the plane when I flied back from the business trip in Myanmar. The rising sun is just like our future: shining, full of possibilities.

In the future I want to be a person with self-discipline, executive ability and logic. Because only self-discipline produces freedom, executive ability produces result, and logic produces a system. Most people long for a steady job. But what on earth is a "steady" job? In my opinion, by "steady" we do not mean steady income or steady state of working; rather it refers to having your own strong point and your own core competitiveness, giving full play to your own value in the future career. This is the true meaning of being "steady."

慕晨　Penny
上海理工大学动力工程硕士
University of Shanghai for Science and Technology
Master in Power Engineering

2017年10月份，来到施璐德面试，是我与施璐德的初见。大屏幕上播放的宣传片，让我对这家公司充满了好奇心。

转而到了年会筹备，我们几个小伙伴共同协作，各有分工，年会可以说是我和施璐德真正意义的第一缕联系，也是和未

In October 2017, I came to CNOOD for the job interview, and that was the first time I met CNOOD. I was filled with curiosity by the prom video played on the big screen.

Later in the preparation for the annual meeting, several other members and I worked together and divided

来同事的第一缕联系。

五月份时，参加了办公室插花活动，在繁忙的工作间隙，施璐德注重陶冶情操，培养爱好，这种企业文化让我感到温暖和认同。

实习期间公司安排的培训，让我对CNOOD有了更加清晰客观的认识，也坚定了我留在这里成长的决心。在未来的日子里，我希望可以逐渐成长，尽快为团队分担工作，贡献自己的力量。我没有特别的，只有真诚，努力，和勇往直前的决心，和施璐德共同前进。

the tasks up among us. The annual meeting could be said to be the first real connection between CNOOD and me, as well as between my colleagues and me.

I took part in the flower arrangement course in May. During the busy office hours, CNOOD pays particular attention to self-cultivation of its members and encourages us to develop our own hobbies. Such corporate culture makes me feel warm and creates an mental identification between me and the company.

The training course during my internship gave me a clearer, more objective understanding of CNOOD, and made me more determined to stay here to grow. In future days, I wish I could grow constantly, share the work for our team as soon as possible, and make my own contributions. I have nothing particular in me, but the sincerity, the hard-working spirit, and the determination to advance bravely with CNOOD.

张百阁　Bague
皇后大学土木工程硕士
Queen's University
Master in Civil Engineering

从去年十二月加入公司，到现在正式入职，已经有约九个月的时间。感受到公

It has been about nine months since I joined CNOOD in December of

司的同事有很多优良的品质，他们温暖，拼搏，宽容，耐心，友善。去年年会我负责的拍摄工作，大家都积极的配合我，非常感谢。今年年初正式加入电力组，项目前期，有不适应，有遇到困难，但是电力组的同事都非常耐心和细心的指导我，尤其是 Tina Zhang, Lilia, Jackie。大家也都很拼博，为了投标，工作到深夜。在未来的工作中，我肯定会做的更好，更加脚踏实地。

首先希望自己可以成为一个靠谱的人，事事有回响，事事有着落。这样才会取得别人的信任，在未来有更多的合作机会。第二，希望自己可以多一些合作。合作是一个团队的基础。一个项目，需要的不只是一个人的努力，所以学会和他人配合，才会步伐一致，共同前进。第三，希望自己多一点创新，在做好已有的事情之后，可以有勇气，有能力去开拓新的领域。最后，希望自己可以成为一个沉着的人，可以沉淀下来，冷静的去面对每一次挑战，做每一个决定，带领一个团队，解决问题。

last year. I can feel the fine qualities of my colleagues—They are warm, hard-working, tolerant, patient, and friendly. In last year's annual meeting, I was assigned the task of video recording, and was very much obliged to all my colleagues who were active and cooperative throughout the event. I joined the Electric Power Team at the beginning of this year. In early stages I found it a little hard to adapt to the working environment and faced several difficulties. Luckily, fellow members of the Team, especially Tina Zhang, Lilia and Jackie, were all extremely patient and gave me detailed instructions. We all worked hard; we often worked until midnight for project bidding. I am sure I can do better and be more down-to-earth in the future.

First of all, I hope to become a reliable person, making sure that there would be response and feedback in everything I do. Only by doing so can I gain the trust of other people and have more opportunities of cooperation in the future. Second, I hope I can have more cooperation, which is the foundation of a team. What is needed in a project is not only the hard work of one person. We can move forward with concerted steps only if we learn to work with each other. Third, I hope I can have more innovation. I wish to have the courage and ability to open new fields after fulfilling my duty. Last but not least, I hope to be a calm person who is able face every challenge, make every decision with composure, and lead a team to solve problems.

袁乐南　Rocky
曼切斯特大学高级工程材料硕士
The University of Manchester
Master in Advanced Engineering Materials

我不是一个恋家的孩子，我希望自己是一个勇士可以踏破世界每一处角落。

生活可以有无限种可能，道路可以有很多种走法，但我一直相信一点，不论选择哪种路，都是正确的，因为本就没有对错，每一种人生都有它不可替代的意义，只看走路的人，是否双脚稳健，目光坚定。

从听到施璐德这个名字，就注定开始了一段美妙的旅程。从相遇，到相知，有欢喜也有困苦，就跟谈恋爱一样。但要想把日子过好，既要学会时时处处为对方着想，哄人家开心，做力所能及的事情，又得让自己不停变得优秀，美观，才能吸引住对方，相互支持相互需要才是平衡健康的相处方式。

很幸运来到这里，这是一个充满爱的公司，这是一个拼搏的公司，有时回家比

I'm not much of a homebody; I hope I am brave enough to cover every corner of the world.

There are infinite possibilities in our lives, and there are many different ways to make our journey. But I always believe that all choices of the road are correct because there is no right or wrong in the first place. Every kind of life has its irreplaceable meaning; it depends only on whether the person has firm steps and determined eyes.

It is a destined wonderful journey ever since I heard the name of CNOOD. From meeting each other to knowing each other, there has been joy as well as hardship, just like in love. But in order to have a happy life, one has to learn to be considerate and make our family happy; he must do everything he can, while constantly becoming better and nicer to attract others. It is a balanced, healthy way of being together to support and need each other.

I feel lucky to be here. It is a hard-working company full of love. Sometimes

较晚，都会发现有身影走在后面，每个人都在为当下的事情忙碌着。有时你根本分不清是为自己还是为公司，其实也不需要分清，开拓疆土的人是为了现在的家人还是为了子孙后代？他们自己都不知道。你做了，受益的会有很多人，但这并不是目的，这只是附加值。我认为，做事情最大的价值，在于我们存在过。这是一个给人支撑的地方，我们在前面打拼，如果不回头，或者没有遇到困难的时候，可能都没有发现，背后一直有后盾在支持。

2012年哥伦比亚大学巴纳德学院毕业典礼上的两句话：

"问题并不在于事情是否会好转——事情总是会好转的。问题也不在于我们是否已经有了应对挑战的解决办法——我们掌握这些解决办法，已有相当一段时间了。"

我想再加上一句话：

I go off work late, I can always see somebody walking behind me, who is busy with the business for the present moment. Sometimes you just aren't able to distinguish whether you are working for yourself or for the company. In fact, there is no need to make such distinction. Those who open new territories were for their families or their descendants? Even they themselves were not sure. Many people benefit from what you do. This is not the purpose, however; this is only an added value. It seems to me that the greatest value of doing something is the proof that we did exist once. It is a place that gives us support. We might even not notice the support behind if we do not turn back or if we do not encounter any difficulties when we work hard in the front line.

The question is not whether things will get better—they always do.

The question is not whether we have got the solutions for the challenges—we have had them within our grasp for quite some time.

President Obama made the following remarks at the commencement ceremony of Barnard College, Columbia University in 2012:

"The question is not whether things will get better——they always do."

"The question is not whether we have got the solutions for the challenges—-we have had them within our grasp for quite some time."

And I add one sentence.

"问题在于我们是否时刻准备着做自己的主人。"

我想请大家一起欣赏这幅图片。这幅图既平常又不平常。我从小就喜爱星空。

这幅图片中除了星星,看起来什么也没有。事实上,其中充满了暗物质,那是肉眼看不见的。因此,从一个外来者的视角去看,我们可以用任何东西将它填满:想象力,信念,努力——什么都行。

每当我凝视着它,一切都消失了,只剩下我和苍穹。仿佛我已经融入其中。我就是它的主人。我总是用想象力将它填满。

我们的人生亦复如是。我们可以用任何东西将它填满,但永远不要忘了还有"美"。它就像星星一样,永远就在那里。

"The question is whether we are ready to be in charge of ourselves every time, every moment."

I would like to share this picture. It is usual and unusual. I love starry sky since I'm a child.

The picture is star with nothing. Actually, it's full of dark matter, that's invisible. So from the outside, we can fill it with anything, imagination, faith, efforts, anything we choose.

When I look into it, everything is gone, only me and the sky. It seems like I'm a part of it. I'm in charge of it. I always fill imaginations in it.

Same to our life. We can fill anything in life, but never left beauty in it. Like the stars, it's always there.

万诗琦　Siki
内部里哈大学旅游公司管理及工商管理硕士
Universidad Antonio de Nebrija
Master in Tourism Business Management & MBA

我是一个特别热爱旅行的人，假期通常会和朋友们约上一起去体验不一样的文化与美景。旅行途中有结识了新朋友的开心，也有因走错机场差点误了航班的惊险；有尝到特色美食的欣喜，也有被海胆扎伤的痛苦。但是，不管旅途中遇到了什么困难，只要能平安回家，我都把它当做对我的考验。就像人生路上，没有谁能一帆风顺的，正因为有这种乐观的心态，我才能从容地面对每一次挑战。而人生就是充满了这些不确定性，才变得立体与有趣。

来到施璐德，我学习到的都是我从未接触过的东西，从询价报价到整理投标文件，从面对陌生文件时不知从何下手到慢慢掌握其中的规则，当然接下来还有更多的东西等着我去探索与学习。

最重要的是，我收到了最重要的职业建议。Dennis 有句口头禅：做最好的自己。

I am a person particularly fond of travelling. In vacations I usually set out with my friends to experience different cultures and sceneries. During the trips, I had the joy of making new friends as well as the adventure of going to the wrong airport; I had the surprise of tasting the local food, as well as the pains of being hurt by urchin. However, whatever difficulties I encountered in the trip, as long as I went back home safely, I take it as a test for me. No one has a journey in life which is always smooth. It is with this kind of optimism that I have been able to face every challenge with ease. And life just becomes enriched and interesting because of these uncertainties.

Since I came to CNOOD, what I have learned is what I never knew, from quotation to bids documenting, from the perplexity when I see an unfamiliar document to gradually grasping the know-how in it. Of course, there is much more to be learned in the future.

Most importantly, I have received the most valuable advice for my career.

我的理解是建立自己的名声。这里的名声不是指的沽名钓誉，而是每一次演讲，每一份工作，都要在能力范围内做到至善至美。凡事糊弄人的人，是走不远的。我也始终相信，你的认真不会默默无闻，而你的成功也不是一次巧合。

Dennis always says, "Be your best self." I understand it as "building your own reputation." By "reputation" I do not mean seeking fame, but trying to be perfect to the best of your ability in every public speech you make and every job you do. Those who fiddle with things won't go far. I always believe that your earnest work will not be forgotten, and your success won't be a coincidence.

CEO 李燕飞女士致辞

Speech by Fay Lee, CEO

  CEO 李燕飞女士首先代表 CNOOD 大家庭以"最热烈最温暖最大的拥抱"欢迎新同事入职，同时感恩新同事对公司的信任，把自己的未来与梦想同 CNOOD 系到了一起，让我们成为同舟共济的一家人。

  她说，作为施璐德的"老人"，我们每一个人都要有这样一个意识：我们迎来了新的家人，我们有了更多的责任——我们需要更努力更勇敢地开拓，为后来者创建更广阔的平台，我们需要更包容更专业的自己，从而帮助他们成长发展，做他们

  Fay Lee, CEO of CNOOD ASIA LIMITED, welcomes our new colleagues by "the warmest and biggest hug" on behalf of CNOOD. Meanwhile, she thanks the new colleagues for their trust on the company and their decision to link their future and dreams with CNOOD. She encourages all of us to become members of a big family who share the same destiny.

  As the veterans of CNOOD, she says, we shall be aware that we are now accepting new family members and assuming more responsibilities on our shoulders—We shall make more efforts to break new ground and build a broader

最强大的后盾。因为有这样一个大家庭，他们将更敢于去学习，去尝试，最终沿着努力的方向，实现自己的梦想。

随后，李燕飞女士一一回应了每一位新同事的分享。"专注，专业，耐心"，"以新人的态度去学习，而不是新人的心态来做事"，"自律，执行力，逻辑"，"靠谱，合作，创新，沉稳"，"互相包容，互相成全，互相成就"，"温暖的大家庭"，"这是一个拼搏的公司，奋斗，做好当下"，"Build your own reputation"。这些新同事分享的未来成长规划，已然是入职最完美的励志语。

她邀请全体同仁一起"重温初心"，回想曾经开启职业生涯的信念与理想，不忘初心，用最快的速度，做最好的自己！一起奋斗，把自己和公司做到更好，彼此成就！

platform for newcomers. We should become more broadminded and possess more expertise in order to help them grow and provide them with strong support. Because of such a big family, they will be more courageous to learn and try, finally achieving their dreams along the way they have endeavored.

Fay then responds to every new colleague regarding what he/she has shared: "devotion, expertise and patience", "learn as a newcomer but not work as a newcomer", "self-discipline, executive ability and logic", "being reliable, cooperative, innovative, calm", "Pristine Simplicity, Amorphous Unity, Reciprocal Constancy", "a warm family", "a hard-working company where everyone is doing a good job for the present moment", "build your own reputation"—Their plans for future growth as shared in their presentations are indeed perfect catchwords for newcomers.

To conclude, Fay invites all colleagues to "re-examine the original aspiration" and review our convictions and ideals that once helped start our careers. She urges us to stay true to our original aspiration and become the best self as soon as possible. She said, "Let's work together and optimize both CNOOD and ourselves, while fulfilling each other!"

带教导师寄语并为新同事颁发聘书

Messages from Tutors and the presentation of appointment letters to new colleagues

谭锦明
香港分公司总经理
Benjamin Tam
General Manager, CNOOD Hong Kong

香港同事 Ben 送给在场的所有同事：

"既有典常，入神致用；不可为典要，为唯变所适。"

"藏器于身，待时而用。"

Ben 引用前一天新同事做 FIDIC 学习分享的例子，通俗易懂地给所有同事们传递了这两句话的重要之道：既有典常，"典常"指每个行业独特的规范和法则，即有方有道。"入神致用"为内心彻底明白到规范和典籍之"微"处，从而达到"用"的效果。于此同时，又不可受到典籍的完全规范，要在规范之上，随顺实际环境而变化，因典籍是固有的，而环境

Ben from CNOOD Hong Kong shares with all colleagues the following quotations from the *Book of Changes*:

"It does supply a constant and standard rule; and by entering into the inscrutable and spirit-like in them, we attain to the largest practical application of them. Nothing can be regarded as a model or a doctrine and only change is what the *Book of Changes* intends to indicate."

"A man of honor keeps his talent to himself and does not use it till the right time comes."

Citing what our new colleagues shared in FIDIC learning the previous day, Ben explains to us in an easy-to-understand way the meaning of the above quotations: a "constant and standard rule" refers to the unique norms and laws of every industry, with its own methodology and way. "by entering into the inscrutable and spirit-like in them, we attain to the

 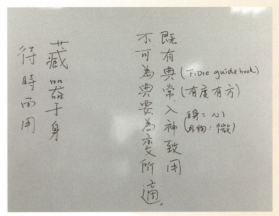

是千变万化的，在典籍之上加上自己的判断。将所有的知识"藏器于身"，成为自己的一部份，随时便可以运用出来。

largest practical application of them", because we have gained a thorough understanding of the norms and the finest point of the classics, thus able to achieve the full effect of application. At the mean time, however, we should not be completely confined by the classics; we should adapt to the circumstances and make necessary changes beyond the norms, for the classics are invariable and yet the circumstances are always changing. We should add our own judgment to the classics. As for the knowledge, one should "keep it to himself" and integrate in into himself, able to use it whenever is needed.

许秋石
业务一部总监
Tina Xu

Tina Xu 感性地同大家分享了她柔软的内心：

其实我一直觉得我们是没有团队之分的，团队更多是指项目的团队或者相对集中学习的小组，其实公司是一个大的团队，大家可以学习不同的小组和个人的优点，可以有更多的合作组合。每个人都努力地成长，你们的目标是成为一个更好更优秀的人，走出团队，甚至是走出公司。我们（"老人"）也一样去努力，希望还能够去支撑你们，还能够一起并肩。这里是一个相互欣赏、关爱、共同成长的氛围。Dennis 把公司看成子女一样，看着他成长，看着他远去。我很欣赏如此的大格局，但也一直有在思考公司和家庭真的是完全一样的吗？我目前的理解是，这是要从两个层面来看，第一个层面：父母给予子女的一定是无条件的包容和爱，引导和支持子女的不断成长，而子女也应该理解和接受父母的不完美。父母的包容和关爱是非常非常重要的，子女的理解也是非常重要的。从这个层面施璐德作为公司和家庭是一样的。但是施璐德的本质是公司，面临的是市场，所以，公司和家庭又不一样。双方都要有很强的责任和义务，保证公司这个大家庭在市场的长久的竞争力。家庭是不可以选择的，但是公司是可以选择的。所以在你们实习阶段的时候，让你们用心感受和选择，确定这是否是一个你们发自内心认可的的公司，是否是一个你们内心会充满激情面对的行业。这个选择很重要，只有确定了内心所向，你才能是快乐的，有长久的激情去经历和努力的。但是一旦确定了自己的选择，要面临的就是责任。公司有责任和义务给予你们足够的平台和空间发展，但是你们也一定要有这个责任和力量去支撑公司在市场不断得

Tina Xu shared with us emotionally her soft inner part:

"It always seems to me that for us there is no distinction of different teams. By 'team' we usually mean a project team or a study group. As a matter of fact, a company is a big team in which we can learn the strong points of different groups and individuals and form more cooperative combinations. Everyone is trying hard to grow; you must aim to become a better person and go out of the team—even the company. We as veterans will also try hard to support you and walk side by side with you. Here at CNOOD we have an atmosphere in which people appreciate each other, love and care for each other, and grow together. Dennis considers the company as his kid, seeing him grow up and then gradually go away. I have always admired his broadmindedness; however, there is a question I have been mulling over for a long time: Are a company and a family really the same in nature? As I understand it now, the question should be analyzed in two dimensions: First, what parents give their kids is unconditional forgiveness and love, leading and supporting them in continued growth, while kids should understand and accept the imperfection of their parents. The forgiveness and love on the part of the parents are equally important as the understanding on the part of the kids. In this sense we say that CNOOD is at the same time a company and a family. Nevertheless, CNOOD is

发展。去认识到公司也许现阶段还不完美，通过自己的努力去弥补，彼此成长为更好。

原先的我很想给大家不断交流分享经验，但是现在觉得我的经验并没有去过你们的未来，而且你们每一个人都那么的个性，都有着不同的优点，我不知道我的经验对于每个你们是否都适用。所以现在的我希望大家以一个包容开放的心态，一起努力往前走，随时交流。每个人都在，你

essentially a company for the first place and is therefore required to face the market, thus quite different from a family. In a company both parties have strong senses of responsibility and obligation to ensure a lasting competitive edge in the market. One cannot choose the family he is born, but he can choose the company he works for. During your internship, you are encouraged to feel and make a choice with your heart, making sure it is a company that you accept from the bottom of your heart and it is an industry that you will face with absolute passion. It is a critical decision to make, for you will be a happy person and have the passion to work hard for a long period of time only if you have decided on what you really longing for. Once you have decided, you have to take on the responsibilities. The company has the obligation to provide you with a platform and space big enough for personal development, while you have the obligation to support the company for its sustained development in the market. The company might not be perfect in the present stage, and you can make up for its imperfections by your effort, helping it to become a better company while becoming a better person yourself."

"I used to be fond of sharing experience with you, but I am now aware that my experience has not been to your future. Every one of you is so unique with your own strong point, I wonder whether my experience applies to you as individuals. So now I hope

们在，我们也在，任何问题，你要相信你身后有人，身边有人就可以了。

最后，一定要做一个追随内心的人，快乐的人，这很重要。

that all of you, with an open frame of mind, move forward hand in hand while communicating with each other whenever needed. You are here, and we are here—everyone is here. Whatever problems you might face, just remember you have someone behind you, and someone beside you. That's enough."

"To conclude, remember to be a happy person who follows the heart. That's important."

张丽萍
合伙人
Tina Zhang
Partner

Tina Zhang 分享了她对新同事的期许：

见到各位，我有一种长江后浪推前浪的紧迫感，看到这么优秀的新人，我会思考我能不能很好得陪大家成长。我也是带着成长的紧迫感去和大家交流，我希望看得更远，才能指引到大家。同时，我又有一种江山代有人才出的欣慰，看到这么有冲劲的你们，我们感觉身体如注入了新的血液，更有向上的后劲了。特别是 Rocky 第一次去出差的时候，他一个人去缅甸和当地对接，打印标书，去另一个城市的农业部去投标，处理得很好，也得到了锻炼，令我们有种后继有人的感觉，新人强，则公司会更强。在开拓市场方面，我

Tina Zhang expresses her expectations of new colleagues:

"When I see you all, I have got a sense of urgency, a feeling that "new generations always excel the old." Having so excellent new colleagues as you, I cannot help thinking about whether I am able to do a good job in accompanying you in your growth. I am communicating with you out of an eagerness for growth; I hope to take a longer view in order to give you proper guidance. At the same time, I am proud that we have so many talents, just as the sayings goes, "Every generation breeds talented people of its own". I feel

对男同事和女同事的带教方式是不一样的,但是爱是一样的。对男孩子,是要求他们能够独立,要培养独自出去创天下的能力,要骁勇善战。我不会给予你我的思想,我只会给你平台、资源,我可以把我所有的东西都奉献出来,但是你们不能一直跟着我的思路来思考问题,你们要有自己的思路去解决问题,要有独立解决问题的能力,要能去开疆拓土。对女同事的带教,我们会更多爱护一些,给她更多的支持,让她知道她不是一个人在战斗,让她先学会保护自己,让她们知道背后有支撑,有后台,更勇敢更自信的去做事情,去判断事情,并且做出最正确的选择。同时,我希望你们能努力去成长,用最快的速度,用身边所有的资源帮助自己成长。

as if new blood was injected in me and I am greatly motivated for further self-enhancement when I see you who are all so energetic. I want to mention here the example of Rocky's first business trip during which he flied to Myanmar by himself to work with local partners, prepared the bidding documents and then went to another city to submit the bid to the Ministry of Agriculture. He did an excellent job, and his abilities were greatly improved. We have the feeling that we have got qualified new members for the future. A company will be strong if its new members are strong. I have adopted different tutorship methods for boys and girls in opening new markets. Boys are required to be independent and develop the ability to go out by himself with a fighting spirit. I will not give you my thought, but only the platform and resources you need. I can offer you all that I have, but you cannot always think as I do. You should learn to think by yourself and solve problems. You must have the ability to solve problems by yourself and break new ground. As for girls, I tend to be more protective, and give them more support. They will know that they are not fighting alone. I will teach them to protect themselves and let them know that they have support and backing behind them. They are encouraged to do things and make judgment and the right decision more courageously and confidently. Meanwhile I hope that you will try hard to grow as

我们因你们感到很骄傲，感到更有力量。初入职场，希望你们将来能自己走出去，有责任，有担当，做一个能战擅守的一个勇士，做一个对社会、对家庭、对自己有责任的人。同时也希望你们能够脚踏实地的，一步一步地做好自己，打造好自己的品牌。

我们一起努力，做最好的自己。还是那句话，任何时候，我的资源就是你们的资源，我永远是你们的后台，如果说你们需要什么支持，我一定会尽去全部去支持你们，你们要记得，你们的身后永远有Fay，Dennis等等所有的支持，所以一定要勇敢地去承担、去开拓，让人生更有意义。

soon as possible with all the resources available."

"We feel proud and more powerful because of you. Now you have just started your career, I hope in the future you are able to go out by yourself with a sense of responsibility. Be a brave fighter who is good at attacking as well as defending, and a person responsible to the society, family and yourself. In the meanwhile, I hope that you can be down-to-earth, become a better person step by step, and build your own reputation."

"Let's work together and try to be your best self. As I have always said, my resources are your resources at any time, and I will always be your backing; if you need any support, I will do my best to support you. Please remember you always have Fay, Dennis and other people behind you. So be brave and go out to take on responsibilities and break new ground, making your life more meaningful."

同事寄语 & 祝福

Messages and blessings from senior colleagues

Carol

学习的真谛是让我们具备发现问题，定义问题，研究问题和解决问题的能力。这个过程和内在的逻辑比问题本身更重要，更需要留心培养。工作是专业和兴趣的结合和平衡，和终身学习并不冲突。无论从事哪个行业，加入哪个公司，通过不断学习获得个人核心竞争力（实力内核—Raven）才是真正的"稳定"。施璐德持续地提供这样一个行业平台和学习乐园，相信 Raven 一定可以在实战中不断接近自己的目标，有所体悟。

从加入施璐德开始，Dennis 和 Tina Xu 就告诉我，团队是我身后最坚定的支持，要学会和团队配合，要做好团队培养。我努力在工作中不断学习，积累和调整自己。作为公司的"老人"，我愿意将自己的所学和体悟分享给每个新进的同事。也希望新同事更快的完成学生和职场人的角色转变，以"职场老人"来要求自己，用最快的速度，做最好的自己。

Carol

"The true meaning of learning is to give us the ability of discovering, defining, studying and solving problems. The process of developing such an ability and the inherent logic are even more important than the problems themselves. As the combination and balance of professional expertise and personal interest, work does not conflict with life-long learning. Whatever industry you are in or whatever company you work for, you can achieve a 'steady' state in its true sense only if you acquire personal core competitive edge (as mentioned by Raven) by continued learning. CNOOD provides such an industrial platform and a paradise for leaning. I believe that Raven will be closer and closer to his goal and get a better understanding of what I said."

"Since I joined CNOOD, Dennis and Tina Xu have always told me that the team is the firmest backing behind me, and that I should learn to cooperate with the team and do my best to build a strong team. I have tried my best to learn in my job, make accumulation and adjust myself. As a veteran in the company, I am willing to share what I have learned and what I have understood with all our new colleagues. I hope that you can complete the transformation from a graduate student to a professional more quickly.

You must set requirements for yourself as a 'veteran,' becoming the best self as soon as possible."

Charles

听了每个人的成长经历和感悟分享，相信随着你们在公司的时间和经验的累积，你们会理解公司这样一个平台化的概念。在这里，我们每个人都希望其他人越来越好。

Charles

"I have just listened to your stories about how you have grown and the understanding of work and life you have just shared. With the passage of time and the accumulation of experience, you will truly understand the idea of 'company' as a platform. Here at CNOOD, everyone wishes other people to be better and better."

Andy

希望大家能一直保持一种平稳、向上、进步、成长的状态。

Andy

"I hope that all of you remain steady, positive, forward-going and ever growing."

Tiger

每位新同事的基础都很好，都非常优秀。大家最终选择加入施璐德，说明通过半年的实习体验，最终都认可施璐德这个平台。施璐德是一个非常好的平台，任我们每个人施展拳脚。公司是在不断发展的，平台是在不断壮大的，未来平台一定会更好。但我们每个人也不能过于依赖平台，要时时保持一颗好奇心、创造心，未来是靠大家一起努力创造出来的。希望大家持续学习，保持自律，与施璐德共同进步、共同成长。

Tiger

"All our new colleagues have a good grounding and are very good employees. You choose to join CNOOD in the end, which is a proof that you have accepted CNOOD as a platform after the half-year internship. CNOOD is indeed an excellent platform where all of us can give full play to our abilities. The company is ever growing, and the platform is ever becoming stronger, which will definitely be even better. On the other hand, however, we must not depend too heavily on the platform. Remain curious and creative. Future is made possible by the hard work of us all. I hope that you will keep learning, be self-disciplined, and move forward with CNOOD."

Jenna

非常开心公司注入了这么多优秀的新生力量，希望我们大家在以后的工作和生活中能够更多交流，公司是一个相对开放的平台，我们没有条条框框的东西，需要大家更多的主观能动性去主动加入。同时我们要做到脚踏实地，仰望星空。祝大家在这边工作开心，学习开心。

Jenna

"I am very happy to see that CNOOD has taken in so much new blood. I hope we will have more communication and sharing in the work as well as in life in the future. CNOOD is an open platform without too much conventions and restrictions, inviting you to show more initiative to join it in a proactive manner. At the same time, we must plant our feet firmly on the ground while looking up at the stars in the sky. I wish you happy while working and studying here."

Mary

做一个自律的人，同时把自己当成一个无知的人。不受利益的驱使，更在意的是知识和经验的积累，发自自己的渴望和兴趣去做事情。

Mary

"Be a self-disciplined person while regard yourself as an ignorant one. Never be driven by interests; what you should pay attention to is the accumulation of knowledge and experience. Do things out of your yearnings and interests."

Connor

希望大家能在工作和生活中找到一个平衡，快乐的工作，快乐的生活。不要因为工作的繁忙而忽略生活的乐趣，这样才能长久保持工作的积极性和奋斗的动力。祝各位新同事在这里，能够越来越好，实现自己的目标和价值。

Connor

"I hope that all of you can keep a balance between work and life. Work happily while living a happy life. Do not neglect the pleasure of life because you are busy with work, or you won't be able to be self-motivated and ready to work hard for a long period of time. I wish every new colleague to become better and better here at CNOOD, achieve your goals and realize your value."

Richard：

多思考，注意细节，团队意识；多交流，多读书，多锻炼。

Richard：

"Think more, pay attention to details and develop a sense of teamwork.

Jackie：
无论什么样的事业都是人干出来的，人一定是最主要的。今天有这么多优秀的小伙伴加入，我觉得我们一定可以做成一些事情，工作当中最重要的是找伙伴，找搭档。因为每个人的选择、着眼点、特长不一样，所以一定是有的人走的快，有的人走的慢。大家不要太在意短期的一些无论是好的还是坏的状况。风物长宜放眼量，来日方长，我们走着瞧。^_^

Maria：
希望大家过的开心，不忘初心，有一个目标/计划，一步步去实现，继续勇敢去争取。

Amanda：
多参与，多沟通，多交流。

入职礼赠送

开卷有益，腹有诗书气自华。为鼓励和支持员工持续学习与不断积累，施璐德家庭一直传承着老员工自发向新同事赠送 KINDLE 的传统。

Communicate more, read more and do more physical exercise."

Jackie：
"All causes are completed by people. People are definitely the most important. I believe that we are sure to achieve something when I see so many outstanding people join us. It is the most important thing in your work to find your workmate. Everyone has his/her own choice, viewpoint and advantage. Therefore, it is inevitable that some would go faster than others. So, don't be overly concerned with short-term results, whether they are good or bad. Just as Chairman Mao said, 'Try to take longer views in judging anything.' There will be plenty of time yet. Let's wait and see."

Maria：
"I wish you happy here at CNOOD. Stay true to your original aspiration. Set a goal/plan and try to achieve it step by step. Be brave and keep working until you realize it."

Amanda：
"Participate more, communicate more, and share more."

Gift for new colleagues

"Reading enriches the mind." In order to encourage and support all our members to learn and accumulate on a sustained basis, the CNOOD family has kept the tradition of senior colleagues

感谢今年的爱心小将们：Tina Jiang, Wales, Lay, Charles, Jenna, Connor, Jeff, Mary.

大合照 & 蛋糕庆祝

最后，感谢最帅金牌主持人Charles和最美摄影师南西的支持！

sending Kindles to new ones.

This year let's thank Tina Jiang, Wales, Lay, Charles, Jenna, Connor, Jeff, Mary for their kindness.

Group photo and the big cake

Last but not least, our gratitude goes to our golden MC Charles and the most beautiful photographer Nancy!

施璐德第一期国际项目经理资质认证（IPMP）圆满结束

The 1st Training Session of IPMP at CNOOD Concluded with Success

■ CNOOD News

2018年12月份，施璐德联合武汉高登管理咨询有限公司开展了施璐德第一期国际项目经理资质认证（IPMP）培训，培训周期为7周，于2019年1月22日圆满结束。

本次培训共有25人参加认证，其中22人成功通过国际项目经理（IPMP）C级认证。

一、培训全景

在2018年冬天上海的第一场小雪中，我们开始了活力四射的学习旅程……

本次培训鼓励全员参与，为了不打乱工作计划，课程都安排在周五和周六。尽管是周末时间，每一场培训都座无虚席，

Working with Wuhan Golden Management Consulting Co., Ltd., CNOOD ASIA LIMITED carried out its 1st training session of International Project Management Professional (IPMP) in December 2018. The session lasted for seven weeks and successfully concluded on January 22, 2019.

Twenty-five members of CNOOD took part in the training session, among whom twenty-two successfully passed the C-Level certification of IPMP.

1. About the training session

With the first light snow in Shanghai in the winter of 2018, we began our journey of learning, full of energy...

All members of the company were encouraged to take part in the training session. In order not to interrupt the

参加培训的人员来自业务发展部、财务部、融资部、单证部、DT 部门、技术部、QEHS 部等。

在开课之前，高登项目管理首先对施璐德组织了企业、项目、个人三个层次的需求调研，最终制订以项目管理系统课程为支撑、以施璐德海外工程项目特色专题课程为辅助的培训方案。同时，根据施璐德的项目需求，本次培训特别增加了 2 天课程，用于 P6 软件的学习和运用教学。

company's daily work, all the lectures were given on Friday and Saturday. There was no single seat unoccupied during any lecture with trainees from Department of Business Development, Department of Finance, Department of Financing, Department of Documents, Department of DT, Department of Technology, and Department of Quality, Environment, Health and Safety (QEHS) etc.

Before the session started, Golden Project Management conducted a firm-project-individual three-level survey of the needs of CNOOD. Then they worked out a training program focusing on systematic project management lectures with auxiliary lectures featuring CNOOD's overseas engineering projects. Meanwhile, a two-day course for P6 software was added to meet CNOOD's project needs.

二、培训日常

本次培训共有40余名同事参加，分为5个项目组，以施璐德正在执行的或即将执行完成的项目为案例开展。理论指导实际，将项目管理的知识体系运用到实际的项目管理工作中，协助知识的理解与消化。

2. Daily schedule

More than forty colleagues, who were divided into five project groups, took part in the training session. The course was based on the current projects or projects which were about to be conducted by CNOOD. Theory provides guidance for practice. The body of knowledge of project management is applied into daily work to help us understand and assimilate the knowledge.

临时成立的项目小组，有项目发起人、项目经理、组织工程师、进度工程师、资源费控工程师、风险工程师、沟通工程师、项目助理等职位。团队成员分工协作完成小组作业。

三、结业

忙碌而紧张的培训转眼就结业了……

熊老师思维敏捷讲话接地气儿、揭老师风趣幽默、石老师逻辑缜密、屈老师专业又优雅、潘老师循循善诱、班主任李老师"永远在线"，每一位老师的授课都给施璐德学员留下了深刻的印象，并且给予了我们非常专业的帮助。

班主任李诗宇老师说："经常收到你们凌晨1点发来的作业；有从南美出差回来上课的；有从项目现场回来上课的；也有出差临时请假的……你们是我带过最International、最忙碌、最有热情的一届。"

尽管工作安排很满，但是每一位施璐德人的学习热情更饱满。根据培训期间的课堂互动和作业质量情况，高登项目管理评选了"优秀学习小组"和"优秀学员"，在结业仪式上，潘老师为优秀学员颁发了奖状和奖品。

A temporary project group consisted of a project initiator, a project manager, organizational engineer, project schedule engineer, resources expense controller, risk engineer, communication engineer and project coordinator. With a division of labor, members worked together to finish their group assignment.

3. The session completed

The busy, exciting session was soon completed before we noticed it.

Mr. Xiong, quick-witted, always spoke in a down-to-earth manner; Ms. Jie was the most humorous; Mr. Shi had a highly logic way of thinking; Ms. Qu was at once professional and elegant; Ms. Pan taught us with skill and patience; Ms. Li Shiyu, our class advisor, was "online 24 hours a day." We were deeply impressed by the lectures given all the trainers and received professional advices from them.

Ms. Li said: "I often receive your assignments sent at 1:00 a.m. Some of you would attend a lecture when coming back from a business trip to South America or directly from the project site. Others would take a last-minute leave for a business trip…You are the most international and busiest students with the most passion I have ever been with."

Despite the full work schedule, all CNOODers are even more enthusiastic in learning. According to their performance in class interaction and assignment, "Outstanding Study Groups" and "Outstanding Learners" were selected. At

the celebration ceremony for completing the session, Ms. Pan presented all the "Outstanding Learners" with certificates of merits and prizes.

四、IPMP 认证

4. The IPMP certification

图 4.1　评估师陶老师和贾老师
Fig.4.1　Appraisers Mr. Tao and Mr. Jia

图 4.2　紧张的笔试中
Fig.4.2　Busy in the written examination

图 4.3 案例研讨环节——等待抽签分组
Fig.4.3 The section of case analysis—waiting for grouping

图 4.4 案例研讨环节——案例展示
Fig.4.4 The section of case analysis—presentation

图 4.5 评估师陶老师点评总结
Fig.4.5 Mr. Tao making reviews and summaries

图 4.6 面试环节
Fig.4.6 Face-to-face interview

五、学员感悟

刚开始接触项目管理工作，一直有个困惑未解决：理论和实践，孰先孰后？孰轻孰重？通过 IPMP 的学习和培训，使我真正认识到了理论和实践的辩证关系，即：理论和实践是相辅相成的，科学的理论对实践具有指导作用，要从实际出发，把理论和实践结合起来。

5. What we have understood about the training

I had a question when I started to do the job in project management: "Which is more important? Theory or practice?" After the IPMP training session, I now truly understand the dialectic relation between theory and practice: They are mutually complementing, while scientific theory provides guidance for practice. We should start from the practice and

IPMP 体系中的 46 个能力要素，是对项目管理工作普遍适用的有效评价体系；WBS 工作结构分解、责任分配矩阵、项目进度计划的制定、资源费用的控制等等，都是项目管理普遍适用的方法理论。以上，都是经过大量实践改造过的、经得住考验的理论知识。

IPMP 体系中的理论方法是解决项目管理问题的一个重要的方法之匙。对于个人来说，还需要在今后的项目管理中认识实践再认识，找到一个一个的方法之匙。这些东西，才是构成我们核心竞争力最重要的组成部分。

——业务发展部 Raven

之前一直从事项目的质量管理和安全管理工作，未能充分了解本职工作位对整个项目进程的要求及特点，也未能有效的运用项目管理的工具进行指导自己的工作。通过本次的学习，系统的学会了项目运作的特点及有效工具和方法，为今后参与到项目管理工作带来更多的思路并提供有效保证。

最大的体会：作为一名工程质量和技术人员，无论今后是否能够成为一名优秀的项目经理，但学习一套系统的项目管理知识无疑是你职业生涯当中不可或缺的压

combine theory with practice.

The forty-six ability elements in the IPMP system constitute a universally applicable system for the effective evaluation of project management: work breakdown structure (WBS), responsibility allocation matrix (RAM), project schedule, resource costs, etc. These are all effective knowledge which has been proven by practical activities.

The theoretical methodology in the IPMP system is an important key to solving project management problems. As individuals, we need to find more keys in the future by learning more and practicing more. These are the most important things to maintain our core competitive edge.

—Raven, Department of Business Development

I was engaged in quality management and safety management. I was not fully aware of what was required for my job from the overall point of view of any project as a whole and did not use project management tools to provide effective guidance for my job before I took part in this session. I have learned in a systematic manner the characteristics of project operation and the effective tools and methodology, which provides more ways of thinking and effective guarantees for future project management.

What impressed me the most: For one who is engaged in engineering quality and technology, a systematic knowledge is without doubt an

舱石。

——QEHS 部 Michael

通过公司组织的 IPMP 培训，对于结构化的思维与明晰化的管理有了进一步的认识。同时，之于项目管理漫漫长路，相信这不是结束，也不是结束的开始，只是开始的结束而已。

——业务发展部 Allen

对项目管理有了更深层的理解。它是一门艺术，科学的理念和系统的方法，配合先进的工具，风生水起。

——DT 部 Nick

项目管理是一个综合的，全方位的管理。个人基本素质的培养要略胜于技术素质的培养。

作为一名技术工程师，可能我在以前的项目中只是局限于自己领域的工作，但是在这次的 IPMP 培训学习中，我充分了解了项目管理的四大生命周期和五大过程组，对项目管理的各个知识领域有了更充分的领悟。

——技术部 Kyle

之前学习了 PMP 的课程，是我首次对于国际化项目管理做了学习，了解了项

indispensable ballast whether he will become a project manager in the future or not.

—Michael, Department of Quality, Environment, Health and Safety (QEHS)

The IPMP training course gives me a better understanding of structured thinking and clarified management. Compared with the long journey of project management, it is not, I believe, an end nor the beginning of an end. It is rather the end of a beginning.

—Allen, Department of Business Development

I now have a deeper understanding of project management. It's an art. Scientific ideas and systematic methodology, combined with cutting-edge tools, help you achieve outstanding performance.

—Nick, Department of DT

Project management is integrated, comprehensive in nature. The training of personal skills is a little more important than that of technical skills.

As a technical engineer, I might have confined myself to the work within my own filed of expertise. During this training session, however, I acquired a good knowledge of the four life-cycles and five process groups in project management, getting a deeper understanding of all the knowledge systems of project management.

—Kyle, Department of Technology

I took part in the PMP course, which was the first time I learned the system of

目管理的体系，这对我拜访国际工程公司的时候帮助很大。但理论的知识并不能在实际的工作中起到有效的功用，如何将知识转化成工作中的技能一直困扰着自己。

很有幸公司开展了IPMP认证考试的学习班，在学习中，实际的了解如何将项目有效的分解管理，对于资源的分配与管理，对于沟通的计划与管理。

非常感谢高登的老师们的授课，将项目实践经验与学习有效的挂钩，特别对揭老师的教导印象深刻，如何沟通在整个项目管理中的重要性太大了。很感谢每一位老师对于我们的帮助，也很幸运的通过了IPMP的考试，之后就是知行合一的理念的贯彻了，要通过在实际项目上的有效运用才能学有所用。

——业务发展部 Billy

结束也是开始

施璐德举办本次培训，旨在培养和输出一批掌握国际先进管理模式与思维理念，具备国际战略视野、综合素质高、技

international project management. That proved to be very helpful in my visits to international engineering companies. But theoretical knowledge was not effective in daily work, and I was rather confused how knowledge could be transformed into working skills.

Luckily an IPMP training course was provided by CNOOD. During the course I learned the effective breakdown of a project for managerial purpose, as well as the allocation of recourses and planning of communication.

I am grateful to the trainers from Golden Project Management for their excellent lectures, which successfully combined the practical experience and knowledge learning. I am particularly impressed by what Ms. Jie have taught me. The importance of the way of communications will never be overestimated within the big scenario of project management. Thanks to the help from every trainer, I was lucky to have passed the IPMP certification. In the future, what is left to be done is the unity of knowledge and practice. We can give full play to the knowledge we have learned only when we effectively apply it in the daily operation of projects.

—Billy, Department of Business Development

It's an end as well as a beginning

By carrying out this training session CNOOD aims to foster a good number of high-level project management talents

术能力强的高水平项目管理人才，为施璐德转型成为中大型总包方作人才储备。

经过 2013 年到 2016 年接近 4 年的艰难但始终如一的调整，施璐德初步转型成功，成为可以承接石油、天然气、水处理、矿山、水电、风电、太阳能，以及大中型基础设施项目的总包单位。

今天，我们每一位施璐德人定会不忘初心，砥砺前行，勇于开拓，厚积薄发，用理想和信念做指路明灯，用知识和技能武装自己，乘着施璐德平台这艘帆船，在梦想的港湾里扬帆起航，勇往直前！

with internationally advanced management models and ideas, international strategic vision, high comprehensive qualities and strong technological skills, and gets fully prepared for the transformation into a large-scale EPC contractor.

After the four-year challenging but consistent adjustments during 2013-2016, CNOOD has seen initial success and has become an EPC contractor able to accept projects in the oil& gas, water treatment, mining, hydropower, wind power, solar energy and large-and medium-scale infrastructure industries.

Today, we CNOODers are determined to stay true to our original aspiration and more forward through hardships. Well prepared, we are brave enough to break new ground. We will illuminate our road with ideals and convictions and equip ourselves with knowledge and skills. Riding on the big sailing ship of CNOOD, we shall set sail in the haven of dreams and forge ahead courageously.

百舸争流，扬帆起航
A Hundred Boats Setting Sails in Speed Contest

■ CNOOD News

2018年5月27日，2018年"vivo杯"第六届中国高校MBA龙舟邀请赛于华东理工奉贤校区通海湖成功举办。CNOOD赞助的"上海对外经贸大学商学院代表队"在比赛中取得了第8名的好成绩。我司员工林焕（Connor）、张百阁（Bague）作为CNOOD代表参加了本次比赛。

比赛当天，队员们8:30准时到达华东理工奉贤校区，换上特别定制带有CNOOD LOGO的队服，在简单的热身活动后，队员们上船进行赛前的最后一次适应性训练。

下午正式比赛开始，倒计时10秒，鼓手击鼓，"咚咚"两声后，全体队员，满桨入水。鼓手大喊一声"划"！于是乎，"龙舟争渡，塞旗捶鼓骄劣"。在鼓手的指

On May 27, 2018, the 6th vivo Cup National MBA Dragon Boat Invitational Tournament was successfully held at Tonghai Lake, Fengxian Campus of East China University of Science and Technology (ECUST). Shanghai University of International Business and Economics (SUIBE) School of Management Team, sponsored by CNOOD, ranked eighth in the tournament. Connor and Bague, on behalf of CNOOD, participated in the tournament.

On the day of the tournament, team members arrive at the campus at 8:30. Changing into the team uniform with the CNOOD logo, they get on the boat after some warm-up for the last acclimatization training before the contest begin.

The contest begins in the afternoon after a ten-second count-down. "Dub-a-dub!" Hearing drum, rowers put their oars to grip the water, with the blades

挥下，保持节奏，保持统一的划桨频率，才使龙舟获得更大的源动力；在舵手的领航下，大家"心往一处想，劲往一处使"，才使龙舟在正确的方向上获得更多的加速度，才能越来越好，越来越快！

1分06秒66，是自组队以来的最好成绩，比去年提高了5秒。虽然，依旧是第八名，但是我们超越了自我，拿出了自己全部最大的努力，我们团结协作，同时又与各校参赛选手一起激烈竞赛，为现场观众带来了一场精彩的视觉盛宴。

fully covered. The drummer shouts, "Draw!" And then "all the dragon boats vie with each other amidst flying flags and drum-beating." Directed by the drummer, our rowers keep the rhythm with consistent stroke rate and provide a stronger motive power for the dragon boat. And piloted by the coxswain, all rowers pull together in a concerted effort, giving more speed to the dragon boat along the right course. It is better and faster!

1′06″66—It is a new record since the team was formed and is five seconds faster than last year. Though we still rank eighth, we succeed in outdoing ourselves. We have exerted all our effort and worked together facing the fierce competition with other teams, giving a visual feast to the audience.

奋力前行的队伍　团结协作全力争先
A team that spare no effort to advance
aim to win in a concerted effort.

"百舸争流千帆竞，借海扬帆奋者先"，这也一直是CNOOD倡导的文化信念：只要努力，人人皆有可能；只要愿意，人人皆可争取。相信"天道酬勤"，相信"长风破浪会有时，直挂云帆济沧海"。

龙舟赛起源于2009年，原是华东理工大学商学院为增加MBA班级凝聚力而创办的华理龙舟赛，后得到各高校MBA的热烈响应和积极参与。自2013年起，在China MBA Foundation 和 上海MBA联谊会的支持下，该项赛事发展成为全国MBA龙舟邀请赛，每年都吸引上千名MBA学子热情参与，如今该活动已成为全国更多MBA提供广阔交流平台，展示团队精神风采的一项大型重要赛事。

"A hundred boats set sail, vying with each other; only the brave one will be the leader." This is also the philosophy CNOOD has been embracing: Everyone has the chance if he makes effort; everyone can compete to win if he is willing. We believe that "God helps those who help themselves", and that "a time will come to ride the wind and cleave the waves; we'll set the cloud-white sail and cross the sea which raves."

The dragon boat tournament, started in 2009, was originally the "ECUST Dragon Boat Competition" initiated by the Business School of East China University of Science and Technology (ECUST) in order to strengthen the cohesion of its MBA classes and was later warmly supported and actively participated by MBA students from a good number of universities. Sponsored by China MBA Foundation and Shanghai MBA Fellowship, the event has developed into a national MBA dragon boat invitational tournament since 2013 and attracts thousands of MBA students to participate. Now the tournament has become a nation-wide large-scale event which provides a broad platform for more MBA students to communicate with each other and display their sportsmanship.

CNOOD 非常有幸成为上海对外经贸大学商学院龙舟队赞助合作伙伴，不仅如此，CNOOD 一直都非常注重和高校师生的互动，交流思想，传播知识。例如，前不久刚刚携手上海对外经贸大学成功举办的"第七届亚太地区商学院沙漠挑战赛"、赞助 2017 同济 MBA 迎新创意秀联欢会；2017 年 10 月同济大学 MBA 组织部分在读 MBA 对 CNOOD 的组织行为进行了实地采访与交流。CNOOD 在员工的培养方面的支持一向不遗余力；鼓励员工进修，考取硕士、博士学位，积极参与赞助高校文化项目，一方面，这是 CNOOD 长远人才战略的一部分，另一方面这也是基于深厚的企业文化底蕴的累积，对高校事业文化事业的主动回馈与支持。

CNOOD is lucky to be the sponsor and cooperative partner of the Dragon Boat Team of Shanghai University of International Business and Economics (SUIBE) School of Management. As a matter of fact, CNOOD has always paid great attention to the interaction with universities and colleges, in an effort to share ideas and spread knowledge. For example, it worked together with Shanghai University of International Business and Economics (SUIBE) and successfully held the Seventh Asian-Pacific Business Schools Desert Challenge. CNOOD was the sponsor of 2017 MBA Orientation Gala and Creative Show, Tongji University. MBA students from Tongji University were invited to carry out on-site interview and communication on the organizational behavior of CNOOD in October 2017. CNOOD spares no effort in employee training: encouraging them to engage in vocational training, or study for master's or doctor's degrees. It is an active sponsor of college cultural projects. This is part of CNOOD's long-term talent strategy, and a voluntary requiting support to higher-education based on its solid foundation of corporate culture.

插花品香　邂逅最好的自己

Enjoy the Scent of Flowers, and Encounter the Best Self

■ CNOOD News

1. 活动介绍

时间：2018 年 4 月 13 日

主题：施璐德 2018 年第一次工会活动

——插花品香　邂逅最好的自己

组织：静安寺街道总工会

承办：上海施璐德国际贸易有限公司工会

课程指导：Amy Gu 花艺老师

地点：施璐德上海办公室

2. 材料准备

花：红玫瑰，多头玫瑰（暗红色，玫色）

叶材：高山羊齿，红叶石楠

道具：手提花篮，花泥，玻璃纸

工具：剪刀，胶带，双面胶

1. About the Course

Time: April 13, 2018

Theme: The first event of the Trade Union of CNOOD in 2018: Enjoy the Scent of Flowers, and Encounter the Best Self

Organized by: Federation of Trade Unions of Jing'an Temple Subdistrict

Hosted by: The Trade Union of CNOOD ASIA LIMITED

Course Instructor: Amy Gu

Venue: Shanghai Office of CNOOD ASIA LIMITED

2. Materials

Flowers: Red roses, Rugosa roses (dark red, rose red)

Foliage: Squirrel's foot fern, red robin

Containers: Hand baskets, floral foam, cellophane

Tools: Scissors, adhesive tapes, double-sided tapes

3. 欢乐时刻

在 Amy 老师的指导下，大家跃跃欲试，以高涨的热情投入到插花创作之中，完成了各自的创意作品。插花者在心境上与花融为一体，通过插花表达自己独特的心情和情感。

3. Merry Hours

Following the instruction of Amy, all of us were eager to have a try. We began the floral design with high spirits and completed original works of art. We were emotionally united with the flowers, by which we expressed our unique mood and feelings.

4. 作品展示

折得玫瑰花一朵凭君簪向凤凰钗

如果是玫瑰　它总会开花的

醉眼看花，花也醉

接叶连枝千万绿　一花两色浅深红

4. Presentation of Our Works

I pick a rose; toward my phoenix hairpin you put it.

If it's a rose, it will bloom sooner or later.

Drunk and bleary-eyed, I see the flowers to be drunk too.

Amid dense green foliage the flower is blooming in two red colors: one is light, the other dark.

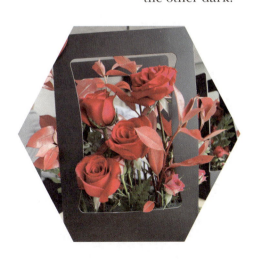

5. 活动合影　　　　　　　　　　5. Group Photo

6. 致谢

静安寺街道总工会

静安寺街道党建指导员　龚老师

F.DATE 花见　花艺老师 Amy Gu

6. Acknowledgments

Federation of Trade Unions of Jing'an Temple Subdistrict

Ms. Gong, CPC party building instructor, Jing'an Temple Subdistrict

Amy Gu, Floral designer from F.DATE

"美在静安 文明交通在身边"志愿者活动

"Beauty in Jing'an, Road Civility with Us": A Volunteer Service Campaign

■ CNOOD News

交通安全
情系你我
文明出行
从我做起

Road safety
Matters for you and me;
Road civility
Begins with me.

为进一步规范行人和非机动车交通行为，静安寺街道文明办主动对接样板路段、区域的市级、区级文明单位和周边居委会，组建文明交通志愿服务队，开展文明交通志愿服务活动。

秉承公司一贯践行的"互相关心 创造开心"的理念，施璐德上海办公室共有12名党员以及2名入党积极分子报名本次志愿者服务活动。

To further regulate the on-road behavior of pedestrians and non-motor vehicles, the Civility Office of Jing'an Temple Subdistrict takes the initiative and cooperates with model road sections, city-and district-level model institutions in civic virtues and neighboring residents' committees, forming a road-civility volunteer service team and carrying out a road-civility volunteer service campaign.

Embracing the philosophy of "Caring Number of Others' Delightfulness, Creating New Ocean of Delightfulness", which has consistently been put into action by CNOOD, 12 CPC members and two activists applying for CPC membership from Shanghai Office

2018年5月30日 上午8时15分，由静安寺街道社区志愿服务中心主办、静安区柏万青志愿者工作室承办的"美在静安 文明交通在身边"志愿服务活动启动仪式准时在静安公园1号门举行。

of CNOOD have signed up for the campaign.

The launching ceremony of the campaign with the name "Beauty in Jing'an, Road Civility with Us", sponsored by the Community Volunteer Service Center of Jing'an Temple Subdistrict and organized by Bai Wanqing Volunteer Studio, Jing'an District, takes place at the No. 1 Gate of Jing'an Park at 8:15 in the morning of May 30, 2018.

施璐德志愿者代表和柏万青柏阿姨合影
Volunteers from CNOOD and Bai Wanqing ("Aunt Bai")

本次活动的志愿者服务队主要来自商务区网格的文明单位志愿者、党员志愿者、青年志愿者及居民志愿者。
The service team consists mainly of volunteers from model institutions in civic virtues within the CBD, CPC-member volunteers, youth volunteers and neighborhood volunteers.

CNOOD 代表队参加静安职工三人篮球赛

CNOOD Teams Go In for Jing'an Staff-Member 3×3 Basketball Competition

■ CNOOD News

CNOOD 篮球少年们在 2018 年静安职工篮球赛中打出风格，打出水平

由静安区总工会、静安区体育局主办，静安区工人体育场、静安区社会体育管理中心、洛合体育发展有限公司承办的"2018 年静安职工体育健身四季大联赛之三人篮球赛"于 2018 年 7 月 1 日，在保德路 88 号洛克篮球公园成功举办。CNOOD 派出了八名篮球少年组成了两支队伍参加了比赛。

赛场上，球员们配合默契、顽强拼搏，在充分享受到篮球竞技所带来的快乐的同时，也有效地增强了整个团队的凝聚力。

精彩瞬间
三分球、抢断、挡拆、篮板球
篮球高手们各显身手，努力拼搏

Basketball boys from CNOOD displayed fine sportsmanship and good performance in 2018 Jing'an Staff-Member 3×3 Basketball Competition.

The 3×3 Basketball Competition in "2018 Jing'an Staff-Member Four-Season Sports Leagues", sponsored by the Federation of Trade Unions and the Administration of Sports of Jing'an District and hosted by Jing'an Workers' Stadium, Jing'an District Social Sports Management Center and Shanghai Luohe Sports Development Co., Ltd., was held at Rucker Park, No.88 Baode Road, on July 1, 2018. Eight basketball boys from CNOOD, forming two teams, took part in the competition.

On the basketball court, players coordinated tacitly with each other and went all out to win the game. While fully enjoying the game, cohesion of the whole team was also effectively enhanced.

Highlights of the Game
Three-pointers, steals, pick and roll, and rebounds
Players showed great talent and went all out to win.